Requiem
for a
Phantom
God

Stephen H. Provost

i

Cover artwork: Austin, Nevada Cemetery, 2022
Cover concept and design: Stephen H. Provost
All interior images are in the public domain.

Dragon Crown Books 2018
All rights reserved.

ISBN: 978-1-7320632-4-2

For my father, who asked the question.

Contents

Praise for other works by the author

"The complex idea of mixing morality and mortality is a fresh twist on the human condition. ... **Memortality** is one of those books that will incite more questions than it answers. And for fandom, that's a good thing."

— Ricky L. Brown, Amazing Stories

"Punchy and fast paced, **Memortality** reads like a graphic novel. ... (Provost's) style makes the trippy landscapes and mind-bending plot points more believable and adds a thrilling edge to this vivid crossover fantasy."

— Foreword Reviews

"Whether a troubled family's curse or the nightmarish hell created by a new kind of A.I., the autopsy of a vampire or Santa's darker side ... Provost's sure hand guides you down gloomy avenues you do not expect."

— Mark Onspaugh, author of The Faceless One
and Deadlight Jack, on **Nightmare's Eve**

"**Memortality** by Stephen Provost is a highly original, thrilling novel unlike anything else out there."

— David McAfee, bestselling author of
33 A.D., 61 A.D., and 79 A.D.

"Profusely illustrated throughout, **Highway 99** is unreservedly recommended as an essential and core addition to every community and academic library's California History collections."

— California Bookwatch

"As informed and informative as it is entertaining and absorbing, **Fresno Growing Up** is very highly recommended for personal, community, and academic library 20th Century American History collections."

— John Burroughs, Reviewer's Bookwatch

The challenge is simple:
Will you settle for the lowest common denominator,
or will you aspire to the highest good?

"How is it that hardly any major religion has looked at science and concluded, 'This is better than we thought! The Universe is much bigger than our prophets said, grander, more subtle, more elegant?' Instead they say, 'No, no, no! My god is a little god, and I want him to stay that way.'"

— Carl Sagan

Preface

Requiem for a Phantom God is the second book I have published in the space of about a month. It's also the second book that deals with the subject of Christianity or, in this case more broadly, monotheism. The first book, *The Gospel of the Phoenix*, was the culmination of a longtime ambition to produce a poetic life of Jesus based on a wealth of sources — some long suppressed by orthodox Christianity. This present work is likewise the fruit of a seed planted long ago.

When I was a teenager, a friend invited me to a church youth group meeting. For the next several years, I attended regularly. It's an experience I consider valuable to this very day. Though I am no longer active in the church — and this volume will provide more than a hint as to why — the experience awakened in me a strong desire to make sense of the platitude being preached from the pulpit.

1

In the midst of all this, my father threw out a question, almost casually, that became the seed of the volume before you. He asked me: "If God knew everything that happened ahead of time, how can you claim to have free will?" Well, he may not have used those exact words (it has been more than three decades now since he posed the question), but the gist of the question stuck with me.

"What do you mean?" I asked him.

"Well, if God knew everything ahead of time, that means it must happen in exactly the way he knows it will. Otherwise, he would not be omniscient."

And who was I, a mere mortal, to upset the apple cart?

I'm not sure why he challenged me with that particular question, nor do I know how — or even whether — he was able to resolve it. A retired professor who once seriously considered a career as a Methodist minister, he now describes himself as a hopeful agnostic. But whatever his intention in asking that particular question, he probably never thought I'd still be pondering it thirty years later, long after I had severed ties with the church I was attending then.

It's been an on-again, off-again topic of interest, and for various reasons, this seemed like the right time to organize my thoughts in print. Some might find it odd that I present such a blunt, rational challenge to the concept of faith on the heels of a poetic work that paints the person of Jesus in a positive and somewhat mystical (if clearly unorthodox) light. The answer lies in the fact that I firmly believe that ideas must withstand the scrutiny of reason, but I also find wisdom in much of what Jesus is reported to have said and done. Not all of it by any means, but a healthy chunk of it. I also believe that, while dogma is often at odds with science, the latter is in no way incompatible with a sense of wonder that arises when confronted with nature. With the universe. And, indeed, that it opens new windows on reality that would have remained undiscovered had we settled for the "safe" yet stifling confines of "revealed truth."

Are we to be the passive recipients of revelation or active explorers of our reality? How we answer that question, in many ways, informs our outlook on science, faith and the essence of life itself. I invite you on a journey to discover how I have answered those questions, and I invite you with equal fervor to undertake a separate journey on your own.

To ask your own questions.

And discover your own set of answers.

"Do you believe there is one god? Good. Even the demons believe that — and shudder."

—James 2:19

One: To Believe or Not to Believe

Do you believe in God? That was a moot point to the writer of James. It wasn't a matter of whether you believed in God; it was a case of what you did about it.

Yet today, nearly two thousand years after those words were written, the question he thought so completely laid to rest remains unresolved.

On one side is the atheist, who insists there is no god. Someone who takes this position immediately finds himself fighting an uphill battle because it's damned hard to prove a negative. Science can show us patterns and explain why things function as they do, based on the best available evidence, but if that evidence changes significantly, the conclusions must change as well. Unless you have access to all the available information about the universe and you're able to process the lot of it coherently, you won't be able to reach any "final" conclusion.

If you had such comprehensive knowledge, however, that would make you omniscient — a quality typically reserved for God. So, in order to prove your point, someone might argue, you'd have to become the very thing you're trying to disprove.

Kind of defeats the purpose, wouldn't you say?

The point is, science doesn't stop. It never rests on its laurels. There's always going to be some new discovery that forces a scientist to revise his conclusion, and *that*, in part is what's scary about science. One day, a newspaper arrives on your doorstep bearing ominous news: coffee is bad for you! But hold the phone: A few years later, new evidence from another study suggests the opposite. It's hard to place a lot of confidence in such a trial-and-error process when religion offers the security of definitive answers.

Consider the penultimate verses in the Book of Revelation, for instance: "To all who hear the prophetic words of this scroll, be warned! The one who adds anything to them, God will add to that person the very plagues described herein. And the one who removes any words from this prophetic scroll, God will remove from such a person any share in the tree of life and the holy city described herein."

Imagine, for a moment, a scientist saying something similar: "A curse on anyone who reaches a different conclusion than the one I have delineated in this research! Now that the question is settled, don't go looking for any new. You might inadvertently come across something that throws a monkey wrench into the whole thing. Then we'll have wasted years of effort arriving at the wrong conclusion and even more time believing it. We'll look like bloody fools! And we can't have that, now, can we? So if you happen to stumble across something to indicate that the world is round, that it isn't at the very center of the universe, or that human beings evolved from earlier forms of life, keep a lid on it, would you? Or else we'll have to put a lid on it for you, understand?"

On the other side of this debate is the theist, who asserts that there is a god. Such a person would seem to have an advantage in the debate, because all he has to do is prove a positive. On the face of it, that's a lot easier than the atheist's task of proving a negative. For instance, if you want to prove that cats exist, all you have to do is produce a single feline and — voila — the argument is laid to rest once and for all. A cat doubter, on the other hand, must search every corner of the universe and produce evidence that the entire kit and caboodle is devoid of felines from New Grange to Alpha Centauri and beyond.

Yet despite this built-in advantage, the theist continually struggles to produce proper evidence. The vast majority of it is anecdotal rather than empirical, and therefore doesn't satisfy the demands of science (more on that a little later). And much of it is presented in the forms of premises and hypotheses that are cleverly disguised as conclusions.

That's because they *are* conclusions. They're written down in the Torah or the Gospel of John or the Qur'an or some other supposedly infallible scripture. And the readers of those texts have already concluded beyond a shadow of a doubt that the world as we now know it was created in six days, all land on earth was submerged in a cataclysmic flood, snakes and donkeys can talk, and a virgin gave birth to the Son of God and laid him in a manger.

Now, the atheist might not be able to disprove the existence of God, but by making claims such as these, the theist has done him a huge favor. Suddenly, he's got something he can sink his teeth into.

Carbon dating and the fossil record clearly indicate that Earth as we know it today was certainly *not* created in six days. There's simply not enough water on the planet and in its atmosphere to sustain a worldwide flood that tops Mount Everest. Donkeys and snakes can't talk for purely anatomical reasons: their mouths aren't shaped in a manner that would allow them to form the kind of sounds humans make in forming speech. That's why they bray and hiss. It's not because they find these sounds particularly eloquent. They're basically stuck with them. And sure, virgins do give birth. Parthenogenesis, as it's called, occurs in some insects, and even some fish, reptiles and amphibians. But it's never been observed among any mammals in the wild.

Humans, generally speaking, are mammals. As far as we know, anyway. So unless Mary was actually a mermaid with a few fishy genes in her DNA, we can be pretty sure she didn't give birth as a virgin.

Unless …

This is the point in the debate where the theist plays what he considers to be his trump card: the miracle. The exception to the rule. The flood, the talking animals and the virgin birth are merely proof that God intervenes in the natural world. "All things are possible with God," is the mantra here. But there's a big difference between asserting that something is possible and proving that it has, in fact, occurred. And make no mistake about it: The burden of proof, in this case, is on the theist. He'll try to convince his opponent that it's the other way around, but if that were the case, anyone could make an outlandish claim and expect — or demand — to be believed. Maybe I saw a purple unicorn riding a pterodactyl over New York at 3:54 p.m. Tuesday, buzzing skyscrapers and singing "Bohemian Rhapsody" at the top of its lungs.

Don't believe me? Well, you should. Unless you were in New York at 3:54 p.m. Tuesday, you have no way to refute what I'm saying. And even then, it's just your word against mine.

The Kangaroo Court

Or let's take something a little more mundane. Imagine I were arrested for attempting to kill my son. Rather than denying the charge or pleading insanity, I gave a full confession … but asserted that I was not, ultimately, responsible for my actions because God had ordered me to do so.

Consider how this might work in a court of law if we were compelled to take any assertion, no matter how farfetched, at face value:

Prosecutor: "You admit you tried to kill your son?"

Defendant: "Yes."

Prosecutor: "You realize you are under oath."

Defendant: "I do."

Prosecutor: "No further questions."

(Counsel for the defense steps forward to question his client.)

Counsel for the defense: "Can you tell the court *why* you tried to kill your son?"

Defendant: "God told me to."

Counsel for the defense: "No further questions."

Judge: "Redirect?"

Prosecutor: "Yes, your honor." (Turns to defendant.) "Can you prove God told you to do this?"

Defendant: "No, you'll just have to take my word for it. It's your job to prove otherwise."

Prosecutor: "That's impossible. I'm not inside your head."

Counsel for the defense: "Move for summary judgment, your honor. Prosecution has failed to prove its case.

Judge: "Motion granted. Case dismissed on lack of sufficient evidence."

Sound ludicrous? Instead of debating whether the defendant had tried to kill his son, the players in this kangaroo court are debating the source of a voice inside the man's head — a voice we can't even be sure exists in the first place. This is precisely the sort of argument theists use in defending Abraham, who famously decided to kill his son because God supposedly told him to do so. How do we know this? Because the Bible says so — the same Bible that's used in courthouses today: Witnesses swear on it to guarantee their testimony will be true. So the contents of the book itself must be true, right?

That's the assumption. But a legal code based on that kind of assumption — rather than on consideration of the evidence — would lead to precisely the sort of comical scene played out in our hypothetical courtroom. It's a fundamental shift in the rules of how we consider the facts and how we reach a conclusion. Anything we can't disprove must be accepted on its face or, as religionists are fond of saying, on faith.

It's as if we've landed in some Orwellian world. Instead of proceeding from evidence to proof, we're assuming proof and crafting the evidence to fit our assumptions.

This is exactly the sort of rule change the theist is attempting to effect in his debate with the atheist. Instead of arguing over whether a man tried to kill his son, the theist wants us to debate whether God told him to do so (which, presumably, makes it all OK). Of course, this is impossible to disprove, and the atheist — if he falls into the trap of playing by these twisted rules — is forced to concede defeat. The theist isn't arguing over whether a snake actually spoke to pair of proto-humanoids, because he can't meet his burden of proof. There's simply no way for him to prove that such a thing occurred. So instead, he attempts to shift the burden by arguing that a supreme, unlimited deity *could have* intervened in history, changed the rules of a snake's anatomy and enabled it to communicate in the king's English (or Hebrew or Sanskrit or whatever language was current back then).

(Or perhaps the serpent's inability to communicate verbally could be explained if he his "tongue" of choice were American Sign Language).

If these assumptions are in play, the atheist must again concede the point. A supreme, unlimited god could, by definition, do whatever he wanted.

Sticking point: There's no more evidence for a supreme, unlimited god than there is for a talking snake. This is something the atheist is not about to concede, and it robs the theist of his only possible route to victory in the debate. Which brings us to the crux of the problem: Miracles, for the theist, serve as evidence that God exists. Yet at the same time, one must *presume* that God exists in order to *explain* the miracles. Without such a presumption, any argument that Abraham received a divine commission to execute his son cannot be sustained. And the only argument the theist puts forth to support his "talking serpent" story is rendered null and void. The burden of proof falls squarely back upon his shoulders to prove that such a ludicrous event could have taken place, and he's left with no case. His only alternative might be to argue that the serpent somehow *evolved* into a mute creature — an argument that would force him to acknowledge the dreaded theory of evolution and, at the same time, would contradict that theory: a talking snake would clearly have an advantage over his mute brethren in the dog-eat-dog world of natural selection.

An Addiction to Miracles

Why does the theist argue so vehemently in favor of miracles, even when such miracles sometimes border on the absurd? Because they're the only real weapon he has in this debate. Maybe it's no more than a slingshot, but slingshots can be effective. The vast majority of the world's population are theists, after all.

A favorite argument comes from the Book of Isaiah: the ways of God are not the ways of man. The intent here is to prove that faith is superior to science. Taken to its logical extreme, this would force us to abandon doctors and seek out faith healers. It would require us to ground our airplanes: if God had intended man to fly, he would have given us wings. It would force us to end our quest for all knowledge after reading those penultimate words in the Book of Revelation. To do otherwise would be to choose the ways of man over the ways of God.

It would also condemn us to a world of irrational barbarism and anarchy, because the "ways of man" inevitably defy the rules of logic that God, as the creator of the world, supposedly established himself.

In his book *The Lost History of Christianity*, Philip Jenkins quotes a ninth century Egyptian monk as saying he found proof of Christianity "in its contradictions and inconsistencies, which are rejected by intelligence and repelled by the mind." So if it sounds stupid, believe it. If it contradicts itself, drop to your knees and praise the Lord. Jenkins further quotes the sixth-century eastern Christian philosopher Yahya ibn 'Adi, who was honest enough to recognize this when he wrote that Christianity "is only received and believed in by the signs and miracles which its missionary showed."

Miracles again. They're a logical dead end, but again, we're not dealing in logic here. What's perhaps more troubling is that Jesus himself is quoted as arguing *against* the use of miracles as proof of divine authority: "A wicked and adulterous generation seeks out a sign" (Matt. 16:4). Maybe that's just one of our Egyptian monk's "contradictions and inconsistencies." In which case, it should be perfectly acceptable to contravene the word of God on the grounds that it is, in fact, inherently contradictory.

As you can see, we've descended beyond absurdity into the depths of pure nonsense, which brings us right back to the point at which we started. The atheist and the theist are operating under two very different sets of rules. On the one hand, an honest evaluation of the evidence can't allow us to fundamentally *exclude* the possibility of a divine being. On the other hand, the evidence put forth to support the existence of such a being is simply not consistent with the world as we know it — no more so than our pterodactyl-riding rock star purple unicorn.

The theist starts with an assumption of proof and thence begins a frantic search for supporting evidence — evidence that only works if one already believes in a limitless God. The atheist refuses to play by the theist's rules. He won't accept an unsustainable burden of proof. Nor should he. He's understandably annoyed at being asked to disprove the existence of God, so he simply discounts it and gets on with his life. As Isaac Asimov put it: "Emotionally I am an atheist. I don't have the evidence to prove that God doesn't exist, but I so strongly suspect he doesn't that I don't want to waste my time."

The result is a stalemate. Each side is intent on convincing the other using arguments that simply don't translate across the chasm that separates them.

In this argument, both sides lose. The atheist dismisses anything to do with religion as the product of irrational superstition. The theist makes belief the litmus test for salvation and, in doing so, loses sight of the principles behind that belief. What's left are two opposing sides defined more by labels than by substance, shouting at one another in different languages, calling each other nasty names and creating quite a ruckus while resolving absolutely nothing.

In the middle stands the agnostic. The person honest enough to admit that the theist's arguments ring hollow but humble enough to realize that there's always plenty more evidence to be considered. Like any good scientist, he's not willing to dismiss the possibility that new evidence will come to light that might support the case for a limitless, sovereign deity. But that doesn't mean he's willing to simply accept the theist's conclusions uncritically and work backwards in seeking evidence to support them.

That evidence is the key. Perhaps if we'd stop all the condemnations and name-calling, we'd be able to let that evidence speak for itself.

That's precisely what this work is intended to do.

.

"There is no crueler tyranny than that which is perpetrated under the shield of law and in the name of justice."

— Charles de Montesquieu

Two: The Audacity of Job

Theists contend that God, as creator of the universe, established the laws of nature that govern the planet and its environs. He's free to change — or violate — them whenever he likes, but if someone on the human side dares to question them, well, hell hath no fury like a deity questioned. Don't believe me? Check out the book of Job.

The entire volume is a perverse exercise in sadism, kicked off when God has the temerity to speak a kind word about a human being. "Have you considered my servant Job?" he boasts. "There is no one on earth like him! He is blameless and upright, a man who fears god and rejects evil." (Job 1:8)

So much for the apostle Paul's infamous doctrine of original sin. According to that badly flawed bit of theology, every person born since our friend the talking snake instigated the so-called fall of man has been evil by nature. Separated from God. Unholy. Worthy of being consigned to the pit of hell. You get the picture. But here, Job is described as "blameless and upright." This can only mean one of two things: Either God is wrong and isn't quite so infallible as he's made out to be, or Paul is wrong and the scripture supposedly *inspired* by God is discredited. Either way, it's another one of our Egyptian monk's "contradictions and inconsistencies" that's impossible to resolve. You can't have it both ways, though Christian fundamentalists will try until they're blue in the face.

(Incidentally, there are other instances that invalidate Paul' absurd claim. Most notably, the author of Ezekiel states unequivocally that "the one who sins is the one who will die" and "the child will not share the guilt of the parent." Either Ezekiel's right or Paul is. Out of fairness and a sense of personal responsibility, I'm firmly on the side of Ezekiel.)

But back to the Book of Job. Having boasted so highly of Job, God finds himself confronted by someone called Satan — a title that, in this context, merely means "the adversary"; nowhere in this work is he even remotely associated with our friend the verbose snake. He has the audacity to challenge God's assessment of the situation and present him with the Old Testament version of a double-dare. He tells God that Job is only living a holy and ethical life because God has blessed him. Take away his possessions, and he'll crack. Allow him to fall ill, and he'll show his true colors. Kill his family and he'll rage against the Almighty.

Any ethical person would simply dismiss such a challenge as sadistic and mean-spirited. But God actually takes the bait: He first allows his "adversary" to destroy all of Job's possessions. His family members are also struck dead. Then, when that doesn't work, God allows Job to be afflicted with sores from head to toe.

Whose rules is God following here? His own? Surely not. Elsewhere, the author of Proverbs states that "blessings crown the head of the righteous" and "no harm overtakes the righteous." Things don't always work out this way, or we wouldn't find ourselves grappling with the question of why bad things happen to good people. More on that a little later on. The point here isn't to get bogged down in that debate, but merely to point out that Job *was* a good person according to God's own assessment and that, according to Proverbs, God wasn't following his own rules concerning how good people should be treated.

The author of Job's response to that is contained in the latter portion of the book: "Who are you to question God?"

It's not really an answer. Just a copout.

God as depicted by the author of Job gets all self-righteous and indignant when Job — grieving, destitute and afflicted — *dares* to question the acts of the Almighty. "Where were you when I laid the foundations of world?" he demands. "Can you raise up the clouds and call forth a flood of waters to cover you?" That's just a brief sample of the defensive posturing that occurs during a prolonged rant the author attributes to God.

Translation: Don't question authority.

With Friends Like These …

It would be bad enough if God, as depicted here, were simply invoking the age-old parental reason, "because I said so!" But the problems here go far beyond that. Foremost among them is the fact that God sits back meekly and allows his so-called adversary to challenge him, then goes all fire-and-brimstone when his most loyal follower dares to do the same thing. So God, as depicted here, is someone who trusts his adversaries and is paranoid about being screwed over by his friends. Setting a fine example, he is

To top it all off, *he doesn't have any reason to be paranoid.* The God of the Bible is supposed to be all-knowing, which means he has more than a clue about the nature of Job's character. Exactly what is God trying to prove here? And to whom is he trying to prove it? Himself? (Is he that insecure about his own omniscience?) Satan? Why should he care what Satan thinks? If anything, he should have gone ballistic on Satan for doubting his word rather than reserving his wrath for the faithful and unsuspecting Job. With friends like God as he's depicted here, it would seem you're better off being labeled an enemy.

Perhaps the most troubling thing about this account is its lack of internal consistency. God is depicted as a paranoid ruler with anger issues who is easily manipulated into attacking his most faithful friend. This kind of behavior might have been typical of petty Middle Eastern kings and tribal chieftains during the period this work was written (there are plenty of examples of such rulers in the Bible itself). But it's hardly fitting conduct for the creator of the universe. It's not a particularly effective style of governance, either. Rulers who turn on their friends and allow themselves to be manipulated by their adversaries typically don't last long on the throne.

Many readers have come away from reading the Book of Job thinking that character's main complaint against God is, "Why me?" But the more accurate question to place upon his lips is, perhaps, "How could you?"

By the end of the book, we don't know anything new about Job. He remains, as always, the faithful servant. We do, however, know a lot more about how the author of the book viewed God. The God of Job personifies the theist's argument that "the ways of God are not the ways of men." Don't question them. Don't try to understand them. They're far too grand for your puny minds to absorb, and they don't operate according to the laws of reason as you understand them. God made the rules and can change them at any time, without notice, and then proceed to change them back again.

This is positive in one respect, because it allows God to do miracles. He can supposedly decide that he doesn't want a disease to take its natural course and stop it in its tracks. He can cleanse lepers, cause the blind to see, send cancer into remission on a whim. But this capriciousness cuts both ways. He can just as easily allow Job's family and livestock to be stricken dead at a single word, or cover him with open sores that are impossible to bear.

Such a portrait of God is, in a way, natural. It explains the unpredictable nature of the world around us while allowing us to maintain the illusion that someone's in control. It would have been only natural for early, agrarian states to form such a picture of God in their minds, modeled to some extent after the tribal overlords and tyrant kings who rose to power during that period in history. Even a capricious, despotic monarch in the clouds is, in a sense, better than nothing. Or more reassuring. The idea that we might be on our own in a vast, unforgiving universe can be intimidating at best, terrifying at worst. At least with a deity on our side, we can appeal to a higher authority and hope that he might look upon us favorably — if we pray the right prayer, contribute the proper amount to the temple treasury, offer the right blood sacrifice and follow the rules.

We always have to follow the rules.

Piety's False Promise

Unfortunately, following the rules doesn't work. You can pray the right prayers and wait in vain for someone to answer them. You can make the proper sacrifices and still see your flocks and herds wiped out. You can give to the temple treasury and still go broke. Take God out of the equation, and the Book of Job actually presents a compelling case against the efficacy of religious piety. Job was looking for signs of causation where no causation was present. His flocks and herds weren't destroyed because he was impious. They were attacked by the Sabeans. His family didn't die because he had failed to make the proper sacrifices, they were killed in a sudden sirocco — a violent windstorm that swept in from the desert. He wasn't afflicted with skin sores because he had skipped his evening prayers; it was a natural condition — just as we now know an epileptic seizure isn't a sign of "demonic possession."

If we want to explain these things, it isn't necessary to bring God into the equation at all —and once we do, he doesn't really fit. It should be enough to attribute Job's ill fortune to Sabean raiding parties and the forces of nature, but in a society that values piety as a means to success, something more is required: an explanation of how these things could happen to a righteous man. Here's where we get to the question, "Why do bad things happen to good people?" The culture that produced the Book of Job operated under a simple premise: Do the right thing, and you'll be rewarded. That was the expectation. Except in Job's case, the opposite happened. This discrepancy couldn't simply be ignored without endangering the entire ethical construct on which the society was founded. So the author, through his protagonist, asks the unavoidable question, "Why?"

The answer, however, is less than satisfying. God's ultimate "because I said so" explanation is really no explanation at all. He might as well have thrown up his hands in frustration and yelled, "How the hell should I know?" That's the honest answer, because the author of the book clearly doesn't know and, consequently, can't pass this information on to his readers.

We, however, do know. As the Jesus is said to have quipped, the rain falls on the just and the unjust alike. A person's moral state has nothing to do with it. Piety doesn't cause rain to fall; atmospheric conditions do. Impiety won't destroy your home, but — as Job found out — a desert sandstorm can do the trick if the place isn't built on a strong foundation. Once we take God out of the equation, we can identify the true causes of our afflictions. Then we put all our attention on addressing them, without being distracted by expressions of piety that really make no difference one way or the other. In the end, they're just red herrings that take up time and energy better spent on searching for a viable solution.

Does this mean piety, or "doing the right thing," is utterly useless? Not at all. Ethical behavior can have profound positive effects within the right context. It can spur people to help the less fortunate, work together for the common good and strive to understand one another more fully. All these things are supremely positive. What it won't do is change the laws of nature or conjure up miracles from a sympathetic deity.

Just ask Job.

"All religion, my friend, is simply evolved out of fraud, fear, greed, imagination, and poetry."

— E.A. Poe

Three: No Other God

The theist might seem to have cut to the chase by simply accepting the existence of God. Can you picture him there, having cut to the front of the line in the afterlife, grinning back at the rest of us as he hands Saint Peter his ticket to heaven?

Hold on just a minute. It's not as simple as that. Having decided on faith that God exists, the theist must pass through another obstacle on his way to the famed Pearly Gates: He must decide what *kind* of God he believes in.

When we speak of modern theism, we typically mean *mono*theism — the belief in a single, all-powerful god. But that wasn't always the dominant belief. Most ancient cultures believed in a pantheon of gods, none omnipotent but all vastly more powerful than we puny humans. Some ruled the seven seas. Some rode on fiery chariots across the sky. Others blessed the harvest. Still others sent their minions into battle.

These gods displayed varying dispositions, which usually lined up nicely with their assigned roles in governing the universe. The war god was mean and ruthless; the fertility goddess was seductive; the goddess of hearth and home was nurturing; the god of the sea was unpredictable. Some gods were loved, others were feared; others still were to be dealt with using kid gloves because they were volatile or, to borrow from the name of the Roman messenger god, mercurial. Mercury, after all, could bring good or bad news.

Gradually, however, this model — known as polytheism — gave way to the monotheistic view that dominates today. Muslims, Jews and Christians together constitute between half and two-thirds of the world's population.

Polytheists? By comparison, they're barely a blip on the radar screen.

How did this happen? During the first stage of the process, a few gods within various pantheons began to become more prominent. Societies favored those whose functions were most important to their survival. Maritime nations exalted the sea god; desert nations emphasized the sun and storm gods; and in an era when infant mortality was high, fertility goddesses enjoyed strong popularity. The ancient Hebrews ("wanderers"), whose mythos gave rise to the three great monotheistic religions, emphasized the god of war and storms. Early manuscripts show the Hebrews' warrior god appearing in a pillar of cloud during the day and a pillar of fire at night, leading his semi-nomadic people across the desert. When these wandering herdsmen came into contact with settled agrarian peoples, conflicts over land inevitably ensued. In these conflicts, the war god promised victory, conquest and subjugation of the enemy.

His blessing was crucial.

The more important a single god became, the more power his priesthood wielded. Rival cults jockeyed for influence with the people. The legend of the golden calf, related in the book of Exodus, offers us a mythic glimpse into just how this may have occurred. The priesthood of the Sinai war god Yahweh, represented by Moses, vanquishes the priesthood of the Egyptian bull god Apis, led by Aaron, and absorbs it. The victorious priesthood depicted Moses and Aaron as brothers in a common cause, but gave Moses a place of greater prominence while minimizing the role of Aaron. It wasn't the last time the priests of Yahweh would suppress a rival god's cult. A few centuries later, they succeeded in banning the worship of their own patron's divine consort, Asherah, a fertility deity favored by King Solomon. (This should come as no great surprise, considering Solomon reportedly had a thousand female bed mates.)

Considering the nearly uninterrupted record of armed conflict that is the Old Testament, it's no surprise that the storm/war god should have assumed such a place of prominence. The same thing happened in Greece, where another storm/war god, Zeus, rose to the head of the pantheon. Among the Hebrews, however, the priesthood of Yahweh went further. Not content to promote him as simply the most powerful god in their pantheon, they set about eliminating their divine competition altogether. The famous phrase in the Ten Commandments, "thou shalt have no other gods before me," became a declaration that there *were* no other gods to have.

It's not hard to surmise why this happened among the Hebrews but not the Greeks. Until the time of Alexander the Great, the Greek world consisted of a series of relatively small city-states. Athens, the most prominent among them, is famous as the world's first democracy. No one should be shocked to find that the Hellenistic view of the divine reflected their very human political situation, preserving a pantheon on Mount Olympus that was closer to democratic than authoritarian. Judah and Israel, by contrast, were never democracies. They famously demanded that God appoint a king to rule over them, and he reluctantly agreed to do so. Such is the biblical version of things. In reality, however, their vision of God probably reflected the reality on the ground. Israel and Judah were both monarchies, and they came to view their most powerful god as a monarch. It's almost certainly no coincidence that the priesthood first set out to suppress the Asherah cult just a couple of generations after Judah became a full-fledged monarchy. One king, one god. On earth as it is in heaven … or, far more likely, the other way around.

But consolidating the godhood into a single supreme figure was nothing if not messy. Not only did rival cults need to be discredited — and then eliminated — but earlier ideas had to be adjusted to fit the new model. Some texts were so widely known and highly revered that they could not simply be suppressed. Hence, the references to gods (plural) in the creation account of Genesis, for example.

More problematic, however, was the fact that any pantheon is full of conflict. In Egypt, for instance, the sun and storm gods (Horus and Set) had operated at cross-purposes for centuries. They were continually at war with each other: Horus attacked Set from his bark, or boat, and Set ruthlessly gouged out his enemy's eye. It was seen as a never-ending struggle, though Horus was portrayed as the ultimate victor. The bark was the mythic vehicle that bore the sun across the heavens, and the eye was "lost" when the sun disappeared behind a cloud. Horus and his father Osiris blessed the fertile land around the Nile; Set was lord of the barren desert.

This was just one of many conflicts that arose among the myriad gods in the various pantheons of the ancient world. Demeter contended with Hades. Thor raged against Loki. Ba'al made war against Yam. The relationships among the gods were nothing if not contentious and filled with intrigue. Synthesizing all their responsibilities, rivalries and personality quirks into a single figure required a combination of ingenuity and denial. This was the challenge of monotheism. Perhaps the most daunting task lay in reconciling the roles of the more beneficent gods with those perceived as hostile or even terrifying. Around the sixth century BCE, the Zoroastrians of Persian resolved this difficulty by stopping just short of monotheism. In a model that codified something similar to the Horus-Set rivalry, they adopted a dualistic system that pitted the god of light/order (Ahura Mazda) against a god of darkness/chaos (Angra Mainyu) in an unending struggle of equals.

True monotheism, however, doesn't afford itself this luxury. The minute it identifies a single god as the source or creator of all things, it must face the unavoidable consequence of this decision: this single god must be the source of both light and darkness, order and chaos, good and evil.

Various attempts have been made to weasel out of this conundrum. At some point, a lesser being named Lucifer was introduced as the source of all things dark and malevolent. His story is based on an ancient Canaanite myth in which a god named Attar challenged the head of that pantheon, Ba'al, for supremacy. It was really an astrological metaphor depicting the morning star, Venus, attempting to challenge the sun for supremacy in the day sky. Attar represented Venus; Ba'al was the sun. When transferred into a Hebrew context, Lucifer took on the role of the light-bearer or morning star, challenging the more powerful Yahweh for supremacy in the heavens. Like Attar, he was destined to fail.

This all seems fairly straightforward, but it got more complicated as more stories were added to the mix.

Lucifer subsequently became associated with Yahweh's adversary (or "satan") in the Book of Job. He also came to be identified with our old friend the talking snake in Eden. Originally, these were three different characters from three different traditions: the snake originated in Mesopotamian lore, Lucifer was borrowed from the Canaanites, and Yahweh's adversary in Job was a figure in a Jewish folktale.

This composite figure became, after a time, the rough counterpart of Angra Mainyu and Set. Unlike these figures, however, he wasn't an independent entity. Angra Mainyu was evil personified. Set was a deity in his own right, on a par with his rival Horus. But Lucifer was no deity. He was a creation of the supreme, all-knowing, all-powerful god. And because of this, ultimate responsibility for his action rested squarely on the shoulders of our old friend, the supreme being himself. Being omniscient, the master of the universe presumably knew what he was doing when he designed the "devil" and could have avoided the tragic outcome had he finessed things a little differently. Because he didn't, he must be held responsible. The buck stops there at the Pearly Gates. There's really no getting around it: Lucifer is nothing more than a mythological fall guy designed to take the rap for his creator.

What's worse, he's not the only one. Humanity itself is also called upon to provide the big guy with a philosophical alibi. It works this way: God supposedly imbued man with free will, which gave him the ability to rebel against his creator in Eden. When Adam defied his maker and ate from the tree of knowledge, he set a series of events in motion that left his heirs tainted and rendered the world itself corrupt. This theological sleight-of-hand would seem, at first blush, to let God off the hook as the originator of evil. It's all Adam's fault, or so the reasoning goes. He was merely exercising his free will.

But truly free will simply can't exist in the same universe as an all-knowing, all-powerful creator. If God knew ahead of time that his creation would rebel and didn't bother to change the blueprint, he's the one at fault. You don't blame your car if it's a lemon, you blame the manufacturer. According to the monotheist model, God created Lucifer. God created Adam. God, in both cases, is ultimately responsible for his handiwork.

In monotheism, it's inescapable: God is the source of both good and evil. As a result, he's either the most conflicted being in the universe — a two-headed monster continually at war with himself — or he's a neutral force. A virtual nonentity. A spineless milquetoast with no real conviction who is, by his very nature, entirely irrelevant. The author of Revelation wrote of such individuals with particular disdain: "You are lukewarm, being neither hot nor cold, and I will therefore spit you out of my mouth!" (Rev. 3:16). The writer attributes these words to God, but he might have more accurately used them to describe the creator himself. A neutral God is a lukewarm God, an ambivalent entity who, in essence, cancels himself out. Consider the Swiss, with their commitment to strict neutrality, during World War II. Were they relevant? Not at all. Relevance belonged to those who took sides, for good or ill. To use an analogy from the world of sport, if you sit on the sidelines, you can't fumble the football … but you can't score a touchdown, either. All you can do is sit there on your hands, watching others decide the issue.

This neutral, irrelevant deity is the god of deism, which acknowledges a creator who set things in motion but maintains he's no longer involved in the world's day-to-day workings. He doesn't do miracles, reward the pious or punish the wicked. He simply created the universe, started the clock running and then kicked back to watch the drama unfold from the gallery seats. Or he packed his bags and took off for some celestial Bermuda vacation, leaving his creation to hash things out in the factory he founded — the very definition of an absentee owner.

The deists, however, constitute a small minority of believers. Their conclusions, while entirely logical, are also repugnant to the vast majority of theists, who demand an active, miracle-working god who rains fire and brimstone on their enemies and rushes in with his heavenly cavalry to save the day. They're too scared to be left alone in charge of God's handiwork; the responsibility is simply too much or them. They need someone to take it off their shoulders. They need *salvation*. The spineless, neutral god of monotheism can't and won't oblige them. So they turn once more to tribal god of war and storm who led the ancient Hebrews to victory in the land of Canaan. He might be an ass at times, but at least he's got your back.

When he feels like it.

The Gnostic Solution

In the final analysis, it's impossible to reconcile the tribal god of the Hebrews with the universal god of monotheism. That's why so many readers of the New Testament have such a hard time slogging through the Old. All the scheming, rapes, murders, genocidal wars and the like — much of it at the behest of the supposedly "good" Hebrew god — is simply impossible to reconcile with the doctrine of universal acceptance they read about in the teachings of Jesus.

Which is it: Slaughter every man woman and child in this god-forsaken, idol-worshiping village, or love your enemy? It's hard to reconcile those two approaches. The meek and passive god often depicted in the sayings attributed to Jesus, accepting of all but ultimately impotent, stands in stark contrast to the bellicose god of vengeance depicted in the older texts. It simply doesn't seem like the same character. And it's not.

The god Jesus describes is, for the most part, the god of universal monotheism. He turns the other cheek because he has no stake in any fight. He forgives seventy times seven and doesn't judge … because he's neutral. As the creator of both good and evil, he's in no position to take sides, so he sends rain on the just and unjust alike. When all is said and done, he's impotent and entirely irrelevant. The irony is that the god of the New Testament is hailed as the god of salvation, yet he's exactly the sort of deity who's least equipped to offer it. How can one expect salvation from a god who refuses to take sides?

The god of the Old Testament, on the other hand, is no universal sovereign. He's the god of *Israel*, pure and simple. He fights for Israel's interests without hesitation; the rest of the world, if it's fortunate, gets to eat the crumbs dropped under the table. One could expect salvation from the God of the Old Testament (though one might not get it — he was notoriously fickle about such things). And one could legitimately call him "good," at least from Israel's perspective. The Canaanites probably had a decidedly different view of him. To them, he would have seemed like evil personified.

Theists have two choices:

> They can follow a tribal god who fights for their best interests in a dog-eat-dog world of us vs. them. This is the god of salvation and vengeance. The god who takes sides. He'll kick some proverbial ass, but in the process he might kill a few thousand innocent civilians. Collateral damage, he'll call it. All for the greater good.

> They can follow a supreme being who is the author of both good and evil and, therefore, can't or won't intervene in the

mundane, workaday world. Don't ask this god for salvation or miracles, and don't expect him to answer prayers. He's off on his vacation in cosmic Bermuda, sunning himself with the lovelies, drinking a margarita garnished with a colorful mini-umbrella.

The Gnostics, to their credit, recognized the problem. They knew it was impossible to reconcile the tribal war/storm god of the ancient Hebrews with the universal god of philosophical monotheism. So they created a theology that separated the two. The god of the Old Testament was a figure known as the demiurge (literally, "craftsman") who created the material world and was vastly inferior to the supreme god of enlightenment. He imprisoned the pure spirit of humanity in shells of corrupt matter, and he sought to keep the first mortals from realizing their potential by forbidding them to eat from the tree of knowledge.

Jesus, a messenger or avatar of the supreme god, arrived to enlighten humanity concerning its true nature. His heavenly father was not the Old Testament demiurge but the supreme god of light and spirit, whose message he came to share with the world. The demiurge, in fact, attacked him in an attempt to silence him, concocting a scheme to have him killed. But he was thwarted because Jesus, as a being of pure light, only *appeared* to live within a fleshly body. The crucifixion, therefore, failed to silence him; instead, the light of his message was dispersed to all the world.

In the Gnostic model, Jesus did not save humanity through some blood sacrifice, but rather by pointing the way toward illumination.

This model has a huge advantage over orthodox theology in terms of logic. First of all, it recognizes that the tribal god and the universal god simply can't be forced into a single entity. One is "good" (as long as you're on the right side, of course), and the other is strictly neutral. You might as well try to force an electron into the nucleus of an atom. Square peg. Round hole. Doesn't fit. End of story.

Second, it's internally consistent. Jesus doesn't save humanity; instead he calls upon humanity to save itself by seeking enlightenment — or gnosis (literally, "knowledge"). Through gnosis, the initiate ascends through various levels of enlightenment, or heavens, until he transcends the corrupt body of the flesh and achieves a state something like nirvana. It's not salvation. It's attainment. And this makes perfect sense when one considers that the supreme god has no stake in worldly concerns such as miracles, suffering, kings and kingdoms. In such matters he is, by nature, strictly neutral. He doesn't provide miracles to end suffering; instead, he provides a means to *transcend* suffering through understanding.

But as everybody knows, the Gnostics lost. Their model might have been internally logical, but it simply didn't offer what most people were — and still are — looking for: (the illusion of) a quick fix. It required discipline, dedication and hard work. Compare that to a model that markets itself as the equivalent of religious fast food. No muss, no fuss. Just confess Jesus Christ as your personal lord and savior, and you're in. Your Happy Meal includes an action figure of the Apostle Paul and a free ticket to heaven, redeemable at your nearest church. Then it's all aboard your flight to New Jerusalem. Miracles will be served mid-flight, if you've earned enough prayer credits on your fleshly stopover. Your in-flight movie will be "The Passion of the Christ," preceded by the short feature, "The Holy Rosary." Thank you for flying Angelic Air.

Remember, it doesn't matter to fast-food believers whether their religion makes sense or not. They live in a world where reason is cause for suspicion, where the ways of man are not the ways of God. It's an Orwellian world where two plus two really does equal five, black is white and God can be both "good" *and* the creator of all things (including that simpleton Adam and that scoundrel the talking snake).

What do they mean when they say God is good? It's really anyone's guess.

He kills a quarter of a million people in a tsunami? That's good.

He allows famine to claim thousands of lives in East Africa? Hey, that's good, too. Earthquakes? Tornadoes? Blizzards? Plagues? Hey, it's all good. Remember, theists start at the conclusion and work their way backward in search of evidence. They're doing the same thing here: Instead of defining the word according to normal conventions, then testing to see whether God's behavior qualifies, they start by accepting a dogmatic idea of God, then characterize everything he does as "good." God, after all, doesn't make mistakes.

More Orwellian stuff, to be sure. No wonder poor Job didn't have the faintest idea why he was being afflicted, and no wonder God couldn't give him a straight answer.

All this rationalizing may satisfy theists who want to have it both ways — follow a god who is both "good" and the creator of all things (good *and* evil). But it's an extremely loose bandage that only serves to mask a festering sore of contradiction. You can cover it up, but it won't go away unless it's properly treated. Why not try the proper medicine? Start with the scientific method, add a pinch of deductive reasoning and a dash of common sense, then slice with Occam's Razor and serve. Lukewarm or piping hot, it's just as appetizing.

Though it's likely to make some dogmatic monotheists more than a little queasy.

"Is God willing to prevent evil, but not able? Then he is impotent. Is he able but not willing? Then he is malevolent. Is he both able and willing? Whence then is evil?"

— Epicurus

Four: All the World's a Stage

Theists have boiled everything down to the lowest common denominator of belief — whatever that means.

Do you believe in Jesus? Do you believe the Bible is the inspired word of God? Do you believe the revelation to the Prophet Muhammad? Do you believe the Book of Mormon? Do you believe in apostolic succession? In the doctrine of transubstantiation? In heaven? Hell? Purgatory? A flying spaghetti monster?

They call it faith, but it's not as simple as it sounds.

It raises a couple of questions that most people want to avoid. The first, already mentioned, deals with what kind of God you believe in. It's all well and good to "name the name of Jesus," for example, but there are enough different versions of Jesus floating around out there to fill any number of parallel universes in *Star Trek*. The Catholic Jesus supposedly takes on the physical form of a wafer during the Eucharist. The Muslim Jesus was a revered prophet. The Gnostic Jesus, as we've seen, only *seemed* to have a physical body. Some think Jesus was a peacemaker, others a revolutionary; some view him as a healer, others as a magician.

Suddenly, naming the name of Jesus has become a whole lot more complicated. Having faith in Jesus means many things to many people, some of which conflict beyond any hope of resolution. This brings us to the question of the day: How does a believer decide *what* to believe in? This is extremely problematic for the theist, who starts with faith and works his way backward to find supporting evidence.

As mentioned earlier, some theists have objected that miracles form a basis for faith. That view, however, contradicts the authors of Matthew and Mark, who state that Jesus "could do no miracles" among the residents of his hometown "because of their lack of faith." According to this model, miracles don't give rise to faith — rather, they proceed from it. Again, it would seem, the theist has it backward.

But if faith comes first, the question remains: faith in whom? Or what? And how does one decide what to believe?

The obvious answer: It's a crapshoot.

If faith — the conclusion — precedes the evidence, it is truly a blind leap. Not a particularly good idea. As Jesus bluntly put it, people who proceed blindly are liable to fall into a pit. And what's worse, they're likely to pull other clueless souls in after them. The definition of blind faith is simple: It's the kind of faith that leaps before it looks, that assumes a conclusion without first examining the evidence. Yet this is precisely the process that the monotheist advocates.

Not surprisingly, he's less than satisfied with this scenario. It paints him as something of a blithering idiot, tossed about like a strand of wayward seaweed on the waves of random chance. If you're born in the India, there's an 80 percent chance you'll wind up Hindu. In Italy? Nine times out of ten, you'll be Roman Catholic. In the United States, there's something like a 77 percent chance you will be some variety of Christian. So what religion you end up practicing is likely to depend, in large measure, on where you popped out of your mother's womb.

If faith depends, in large measure, on such a haphazard process, what does that say about its power? Certainly, any *true* belief should be able to overcome such petty obstacles and permeate the entire world. It's not as if the Chinese believe that trees exist and provide shade, while the British reject these ideas. A belief in trees and their shade is universal (except, perhaps, to those who have lived all their lives in a barren desert) because that oak or elm is plainly visible and standing right in front of us. We have sensory evidence of it. God's a little trickier. Because you can't see him, there's vast disagreement over whether he exists and what, exactly, his nature is. It's not a harmless little dispute, either. It's the kind of thing that leads to cataclysmic wars that leave millions of people dead on either side of the issue. It is no accident that so many pogroms and genocides can be traced to disagreements over the nature of God.

This is coldly ironic, because most religions include teachings that condemn killing other human beings.

Why should believers so openly defy the commandments of their own belief system?

In a word, fear.

The Devil Made Me Do It

A father who asked Jesus to heal his son reportedly once asked him: "My lord, I believe. Please help me overcome my unbelief" (Mark 9:24).

But just how is this done?

Religious zealots often seek to overcome their unbelief by forcing others to believe as they do. Or, if they refuse, eliminating them. This is not a sign of faith, but rather an indication that they have grave doubts about their own god and his religion. In order to assuage these doubts, they have to re-create the world in their own image — a world with nothing to remind them that they might, just *might* be wrong. This is a world in which heretics are forced to recant at the point of a sword, then summarily executed for fear that their repentance was somehow less than genuine (imagine that). Apostates are condemned to death. Pagans and heathens are converted by force of arms, then "encouraged" to donate all their worldly goods to the church.

Why?

All because these people who claim to have faith feel actually feel extremely threatened by the fact that someone believes differently than they do. On some level, they're really doubting Thomases who must reassure themselves that they're right by forcibly converting or eliminating the competition. They realize that obvious truths (such as the existence of a tree and its ability to provide shade) are, in almost every case, universally acknowledged. Their belief in God, the creator of the universe, should be the most fundamental, self-evident truth of all. Yet it's not. So when others believe in a different God, or a different concept of the divine, it's a painful reminder that the existence of a simple tree is more widely acknowledged on Planet Earth than the supposed existence of the one they believe *created* that tree — and all others like it.

This leaves the theist scrambling about madly, looking for some explanation.

True to form, he finds one — though it's rather tortured and not very convincing. Here's where the devil comes in handy. The cliché that "the devil made me do it" may sound trite, but it's really at the heart of the theist's explanation. Why doesn't the whole world recognize the Christian God? Because they're being deceived! It's all a vast conspiracy by some invisible entity and his minions to obscure the truth from hundreds of millions of people. Satan appears as an "angel of light" to blind these poor, unsuspecting souls from truth that would *otherwise be* self-evident.

This only works, however, if the devil is a free agent. But monotheism simply can't allow this. In this closed system, the devil was created by the supreme being and is therefore simply acting in accordance with his nature — the nature God gave him, knowing how everything would turn out ahead of time. Such a god must therefore be ultimately responsible for his actions, and would appear to be acting against his own best interests in purposely blinding people to his existence. This sort of god is nothing but a self-contradiction. He's the kind of God who tells Moses to demand that the pharaoh free the Hebrews from slavery. Then he countermands his own purpose by "hardening" the pharaoh's heart so that he refuses Moses' demands.

Kind of self-defeating, don't you think?

What makes matters even worse is his stated purpose for doing so. God states that he's hardening the pharaoh's heart as an excuse to perform signs and wonders so that the Egyptians "will know that I am the lord." These so-called signs and wonders turn out to be a series of plagues that pollute the Nile, destroy the nation's grain, kill its livestock and wipe out an entire generation of Egyptians.

Huh?

Would you like to run that by me again?

All this seems a tad messy, cruel and … ineffective. Wouldn't it make a lot more sense to *soften* the pharaoh's heart? Lives would be spared, a cataclysm avoided, and a lot more Egyptians — as subjects of the pharaoh — would wind up acknowledging the god of Moses. If God really had wanted the Egyptians to acknowledge him, he would have influenced the pharaoh to make his cult the state religion, thereby guaranteeing himself millions of new followers. Instead, he chose to go berserk on them and try to "persuade" them by brute force. That works like a charm if you want to build resentment, but it's not particularly effective if you want to win followers. Indeed, there's no indication that the Egyptians took the "opportunity" to convert en masse to the cult of the Hebrew god. Once the Hebrew migration out of Egypt was complete, the Egyptians continued worshipping Isis, Amen-Ra, Horus, Bast, Osiris and the rest of them for more than a millennium.

God comes off as sadistic in the extreme, and a damned lousy evangelist to boot.

This story, however, illustrates what happens when you remove the middleman. Later theologians might have tried to absolve God of responsibility for hindering the Hebrews by blaming it all on Satan. They might have said it was the devil who hardened the pharaoh's heart, forcing God's hand against them. Or they might have blamed it all on mankind's "sinful nature," as it spread from Adam.

Instead, we have a god who goes about killing all the firstborn sons of Egypt. This is almost exactly the same tactic the corrupt pharaoh of Moses' youth supposedly used in an attempt to rid himself of the future deliverer, and that Herod the Great supposedly resorted to in seeking to murder Jesus. That puts the God of Israel in some pretty nefarious company.

As we have seen, however, a supreme god can't avoid ultimate responsibility for the actions of his creation. He knew what he was getting into when he set the mold. Being omniscient, he saw what the consequences would be, and he could have avoided it all very simply by opting for a different design.

But he didn't.

This is the point at which the author of Job starts raging, "Who are you to question God?"

I'm sorry, but if God creates rules he can't abide by, what reason do we have to respect him? Jesus presented God as a role model — someone to be emulated. By his own admission, he did only that which he saw his heavenly father doing. According to the gospels, he didn't go around calling down plagues on people, starting wars or destroying civilizations with cataclysmic floods. But he did do one thing that's consistent with the Moses story: He told his followers: "To you it has been given to know the secrets of God's kingdom, but those outside hear everything in parables, that seeing, they may not perceive and hearing, they may not understand. Otherwise, they might repent and be forgiven" (Mark 4:11-12).

Just like the pharaoh, their hearts were hardened — not by Satan, but by God (or his son/prophet).

Lest anyone think this concept is peculiar to the Judeo-Christian scriptures, a glance at the Qur'an states categorically that, "as for disbelievers, whether you warn them or fail to warn them, it is all the same — they will not believe. Allah has set a seal on their hearts and their hearing; a blindfold covers their sight. Theirs shall be a terrible doom" (2:7).

One has to wonder why Allah or Jesus should want to restrict the number of people following them. The answer lies in the fact that they don't. These sayings weren't meant to be restrictive, but rather to explain the existence of human beings who failed to acknowledge the god of the universe. If God is all-powerful, why doesn't everyone believe?

Any religion claiming to worship an all-powerful creator deity must grapple with this question.
It's part of the inherent contradiction that arises when one tries to reconcile the idea of a "good" god with the concept of an omnipotent creator. Islam, like Judaism and Christianity before it, has a hard time melding these ideas in any coherent sense. On the one hand, the Qur'an sides with the universal god, proclaiming that "all things are from Allah," but in the very next verse, it contradicts this, stating that "whatever good befalls you is from Allah, and whatever misfortune comes your way is your own doing" (4:78-79).

Yet another section shows Allah engaging in the same sort of behavior attributed to the god of Moses when he hardened the pharaoh's heart: "No soul can believe, save by the will of Allah" (10:100). And in another section: "If Allah so willed, he could make you all a single people. But he allows to stray those he pleases and guides those he pleases" (16:93). This anticipates John Calvin's despicable doctrine of predestination by nearly a thousand years and leaves one to wonder whether the sadistic Swiss theologian developed his philosophy by reading the Islamic holy book. The same approach, however, is favored not only in the story of pharaoh's hardened heart but also in the writings of Paul, Augustine of Hippo and others.

As should be obvious, statements such as these eliminate any argument for free will and personal responsibility. They constitute bald-faced admissions that God is, in fact, ultimately responsible for everything that happens — as a supreme God must, by his very nature, be responsible. Not only for healing, but for disease. Not only for peacemaking, but for declaring war. As the author of Ecclesiastes put it: "To everything, there is a season" (Eccl. 3:1). And God orders those seasons the way he sees fit.

We're no more than pawns on a chessboard or cannon fodder in a fully choreographed spiritual "war." The outcome is predetermined, but the casualties are no less real. God is some cosmic version of the mad emperor Caligula, ordering games at the Colosseum for his pleasure and cheering wildly as the participants fight each other to the death. The damage to his reputation as a good and loving god is a steep price to pay, but that reputation must be sacrificed to preserve something his followers find far more precious: their sense of security.

If God is in control of everything, it means millions or even billions of innocent people will be slaughtered in his name and summarily sentenced to an eternity in hell. But it also explains why the pharaoh didn't simply free the Hebrews. It explains why some rejected Jesus' message. It explains why Christianity isn't universally acknowledged as self-evident truth. And, perhaps most importantly, it makes faith seem less blind. Less random.

We don't follow this or that religion because we were born in the United States or Italy or Mexico. Or because, by some stroke of fortune, we happened to grow up next door to a church. We follow because we were destined to do so. Like Israel, we are a chosen people. Like Israel, God fights on our behalf against the heathens who oppose us and, by extension, that oppose him.

Such ideas have nothing to do with a transcendent god of the universe. Such a disconnected concept is simply too scary for the theists to accept. In the end, the realization that a supreme god must be responsible for everything sends them running like frightened children back into the arms of a tribal god who fights their battles for them. They can't bring themselves to put their faith in some distant, neutral entity who remains on the sidelines in the war between good and evil. So they opt instead for a sadistic brute whose divinity gives him a 007-style license to kill. And pillage. And infect. And destroy. Indeed, it gives him immunity from prosecution for crimes that would land a mere human in a jail cell, a war crimes court or a mental institution.

This isn't a god who practices what he preaches; it's a deity whose mantra is, rather, "Do as I say, not as I do."

"It is a most astonishing thing that people can believe that this world … with all its defects, should be the best that omnipotence and omniscience have been able to produce in millions of years."

— Bertrand Russell

Five: Clapton is God

The phrase "Clapton is God" first appeared spray painted on the wall at Islington underground station, a subway stop in Greater London, sometime during the mid-1960s. It referred to Eric Clapton, a young guitarist in John Mayall's Bluesbreakers who was building quite a reputation. Someone took a photograph of the graffiti, which was widely circulated. Soon, the phrase began popping up elsewhere, and it eventually became part of the lexicon. Clapton, for his part, continued to gain fans with Cream, Blind Faith and Derek and the Dominoes, and ultimately as a solo artist.

What does any of this have to do with our present investigation? Just this: We like our gods in corporeal form. That's another reason the Gnostic ideal of a distant, neutral deity didn't find a larger audience. The Force may have been with Luke Skywalker, but Han Solo had the Millennium Falcon and a kick-ass attitude. Guess which character audiences preferred — and which actor went on to become a regular Hollywood leading man.

Mythology is filled with accounts of gods who took on human flesh. Many of them enjoyed the company of human females and fathered demigods with names like Achilles and Gilgamesh and Cu Chulainn. None of them was named Clapton or Han Solo, as far as I can determine. But there was definitely a precedent for this sort of thing before Jesus came down the pike.

It's only natural, really. As an author, I've often been counseled to "write about what you know," and authors of religious texts no doubt did the same. The problem lies in the fact that writers in ancient cultures just didn't know that much — at least not in comparison to the wealth of information at our disposal today. Yet we tend to treat them as though they did. The story of the flood in Genesis is a perfect example. The author set down the story of a worldwide flood that covered "all the high mountains underneath the heavens" and destroyed all life on Earth.

Leaving aside the fact that this would have been scientifically impossible, I have a single question I'd like to ask the author, if he were alive today.

How do you know?

The flood story was originally set down in ancient Mesopotamia some 3,000 years BCE. After that, it went through a few modifications and appeared in various forms, the most recent being the story of Noah in the Bible (in earlier versions, the protagonists bore unwieldy names like Atrahasis and Utnapishtim). So this story dates back some five millennia.

Five thousand years ago, we didn't have satellites or GPS or jets that could fly around the world a day or less. There was simply no way of knowing how far a flood extended, no matter how devastating it might have been in local terms. Unless the author of Genesis had access to a donkey that could travel at supersonic speeds, he'd have absolutely no way of knowing the true scope of the flood. The "earth" to him was probably the Tigris-Euphrates river valley, a floodplain prone to occasional inundations. For us to translate his use of the world "earth" into some planetary reference would be the height of stupidity — and hubris. You know, pride. That thing the Bible says goeth before a fall.

But hubris has long been a hallmark of religion. God (or the gods) look and act like we do. The sun orbits the Earth, which is at the exact center of the universe. Humans couldn't have possibly descended from brutish apelike creatures, let alone single-celled organisms. What an insult! We're *better* than that, after all!

An Argument With a Flawed Design

Aren't we?

Only as we have gained a broader sense of the universe's vast scope have we begun to realize we aren't the "be all and end all" of this reality. We're part of an ecosystem, not masters of it. We might be at the apex, but we've exploited that position to our own detriment as often as not — in part because we have an exaggerated sense of self-importance, a cock-sure bravado that tells us we're created in the very image of God. More likely, however, we've imagined him in our own image because we *can't* imagine anything else. We're limited to the information gathered by our senses, and we can't form pictures of things we haven't seen. We can't ask a child, for instance, to describe ultraviolet light. Or, for that matter, to describe a kangaroo if he's never seen one.

Yet in our hubris, we presume to insist that God can — and should — be defined in very human terms, simply for our own convenience.

This isn't good science. It's raw assumption, and it's the basis for one age-old argument for the existence of God: the argument from design. It goes something like this: "I know that God created the world because it's designed so intricately, it must have been created by an intelligent being. Look at this Toyota Camry. It didn't just come together randomly on its own. Someone had to make it. Ergo, someone had to make the world, too. It's a whole lot more complicated than a car!"

The argument assumes that, simply because humans assembled an automobile, someone like a human *must* have used a similar process to assemble the world as we know it.

It says absolutely nothing about *who* might have assembled it.

"Did workers at a Ford Motor Company plant make that Camry?" I might ask.

"No," comes the answer, "workers at a Toyota factory did."

"How do you know?"

"It says so there on the nameplate."

"Well, it could be a knockoff, but even if it's not, there's no particular nameplate on the world, as far as I know. So how do you know the Christian god created it, as opposed to say Allah or Ptah or someone else? Can I see your copy of the warranty?"

He hands me a copy of the Bible.

I hand him a copy of the Qur'an in return.

"My warranty seems to indicate yours is no longer valid," I tell him. "You might want to see if there's a recall."

Not on the world itself. On the warranty, which seems to have very little connection to the product itself. That's just the thing: The texts of monotheism, which are written in the name of a universal creator, say virtually nothing about the process of creation itself. It's six days and done, then on to the "good stuff" — like rushing through the introductory credits to a soap opera. In Genesis, the creation account takes up just two chapters out of half-a-hundred, and it's actually *two* accounts that defy the laws of nature and blatantly contradict each other. (Most scholars agree they were written by two different authors and then cobbled together rather clumsily.)

In the first chapter, vegetation makes its appearance a full day *before* the sun is created. Now that's a nifty trick, considering plants use a process called photosynthesis that's directly dependent upon sunlight.

Moreover, the order of creation is set down differently in the two versions.

Genesis 1:
1. Vegetation (fourth day)
2. Animals (fifth day)
3. Humans (sixth day)

Genesis 2:
1. Humans
2. Vegetation
3. Animals

There's no mention of six days in the second account, but that's beside the point. The crux of the problem lies in a simple logical contradiction. Either humans were fashioned *before* plants and animals or *afterward* … unless God somehow messed up and decided to take a mulligan. (See the myth of Lilith for a version of this alternative.) And actually, I should have written "the gods," because the text clearly quotes them as saying, "Let *us* make man in *our* own image" and uses the plural noun Elohim, indicating more than one god. One of these gods then appears to lose track of the humans in the garden and has to go looking for him, like a zany mad scientist who's forgotten where he's laid his glasses.

Clearly, this text presents monotheism at a point in the process when it was still trying to reconcile itself with its polytheistic roots. When the supposed creator is depicted as bumbling about like that, it's hard to find much sympathy for an argument called "intelligent design." Yet this is precisely what the monotheists propose.

Let's go back to the car analogy for a moment. The monotheist argues that we're like automobiles: A car needs a manufacturer, so we must need a creator. That sounds all well and good on the surface, but it doesn't prove anything. It's an analogy, not evidence — an argument for the principle of judging a book by its cover. Furthermore, it's an imperfect analogy at best, one that fails to hold up under the most superficial scrutiny.

The monotheist starts with the assumption that intelligence is necessary to create something. The car (or the pocket watch, or the deluxe side-by-side refrigerator/freezer with icemaker and built-in temperature regulator) doesn't come together all by itself. But that just doesn't hold true. The domesticated turkey is notoriously stupid, but if you put two of the opposite sex together, they're more than capable of creating a new turkey.

"Hold on," my monotheist friend will argue. "I'm talking about creating something out of nothing. *Ex nihilo*. Completely from scratch."

"Then your analogy falls flat," I say. "In fact, you can't create an effective analogy because nothing works that way. Our feathered friends on the turkey farm need DNA and a couple of compatible gametes (a sperm and an egg). Our friend on the assembly line at Ford Motor Co. needs screws, a gearshift, a carburetor, etc. So your creator, whose existence you have yet to prove, by your own admission works using an entirely different process. Hence, there's no way to say whether it's intelligent or not … or even whether it has occurred."

Some readers may accuse me of setting up a straw man argument. But the argument from design, as it's called, is not *my* argument. Christian theologians have been trumpeting it for centuries as "proof" their god exists. The plain fact is, it doesn't prove a thing. It doesn't establish that *any* god exists, let alone the Christian god. What it does is provide another example of the arrogance that puts humanity at the center of the universe and demands that everything, including the supposed creator, conform to our idea of how things should be.

Part of this is based on human neurophysiology. A section of the brain known as the fusiform face area (FFA) is designed to look for and recognize human faces. The FFA is crucial in allowing an infant to recognize his mother's face and identifying her as a source of safety. It prompts some people to see the image of the Virgin Mary on a tree stump or the face of Jesus on a grilled cheese sandwich. It also probably plays a role in our decision to depict God as an old man with white hair and a beard framing a very human face — and in our portrayals of various cartoon animals with decidedly anthropomorphic features.

We seem to look for signs of humanity in everything, including our gods. And, conversely, we seem to look for signs of divinity in ourselves.

God created us in his own image, after all — so the author of Genesis says. In doing so, he imbued us with something else: the hope of immortality.

If Jesus can heal a leper … if Neil Armstrong can walk on the moon … if Eric Clapton can make *Layla* sound like better than heaven's most accomplished angelic harpist … then we clearly have the spark of the divine within us. Why is it, then, that we just can't seem to conquer that final frontier? No, not space, dear Trekker.

Death.

It throws a huge monkey wrench into our rather inflated self-image, and it would force us to re-examine our conclusion that humanity is, in fact, capable of conquering it. If, that is, we didn't have faith. And evidence be damned: "Blessed are they," Jesus reportedly told a doubting apostle, "who have not seen, but still believed."

Blessed are they who have not seen? That seems like an apt description of blind guides who lead their equally clueless followers into a pit.

I didn't say that.

Jesus did.

"Disobedience is the true foundation of liberty. The obedient must be slaves."

– Henry David Thoreau

Six: The Eden Incident

Like the fusiform face area, all humans share something else in common: a fear of death. With a few thousand years of history under our belts and some pretty handy powers of observation, we've noticed something.

We all die.

Most of us, however, don't want to — not unless we're suffering from a debilitating illness or chronic depression. The survival instinct is deeply ingrained in us and nicely explained by Darwinian theory. We naturally want to survive so we can pass along the best possible genetic code to the next generation.

Ours.

It's a part of the process Darwin called natural selection.

Death plays an important role in this process. Individuals who survive longer have a greater opportunity to preserve their DNA than those who die young. Barring accidents and bad luck, they survive longer because they're better equipped to do so. But even these individuals have to die eventually, so the next generation can take their place. Changes — or mutations — in genetic makeup along the way can make a few members of succeeding generations even better equipped than their parents to survive in their environment ... until, of course, that environment changes and different skills or attributes are required.

It's a very simple paradigm.

The theistic model, by comparison, is fraught with difficulties. Let's start with the assumption that humans made in God's image should be, like God, immortal. Clearly, we aren't, so something must be amiss.

This requires an explanation. God certainly can't be at fault, no matter how convincingly Genesis portrays him as a cross between Disney's absent-minded professor and Gene Wilder's character in *Young Frankenstein*. The blame must be placed, and it must be placed elsewhere. Not on God ... even though, as we've seen, he's ultimately responsible for everything that happens. That's a tough detail to ignore, but the monotheists do their level best to deflect the blame onto not one but three different individuals.

1. Our friend the talking serpent.
2. The first woman (unless you include the tale of Lilith), Eve.
3. The first man, Adam.

The author no sooner finishes telling us that God created man "in his own image" — and breathing his very own spirit into him — than he's placing a couple of very big caveats on that statement. First of all, this newly formed mini-god isn't immortal like his creator. In order to achieve this state, he has to eat from a certain tree. Second, he doesn't know the difference between right and wrong. Now, that's pretty basic. Several verses in the Bible identify God as the source of wisdom, yet he has somehow neglected to impart this particular trait to his favorite creation. Instead, he has hidden it up *another* tree and (here's the kicker) expressly forbidden Adam and Eve to partake of it ... on pain of death: "In the day you eat of it, you will surely die."

With these two rather fundamental traits out of the way, we're left to wonder in just what sense the first humans were created in God's image. Did they have red hair and freckles? A violent temper? An uncanny knack for running the table in Vegas or winning every game of Parcheesi? The author of Genesis never clues us in. All we're told is that the first humans were neither immortal nor particularly astute. The term "dim bulb" comes to mind.

In other words, perfect targets for a con artist.

Enter our old friend, Mr. Scaly, who slithers up (or walks up — he supposedly had appendages before he was "cursed") and tempts our gullible friends into taking a bite out of the fruit from the so-called tree of knowledge. He makes his pitch by arguing that the fruit "is desirable to make one wise" and that God really has no intention of following through on that threat to summarily execute them if they violate his commandment. On both counts, he turns out to be right. The fruit does indeed reveal to them the difference between good and evil. Moreover, God doesn't smite them dead that very day.

So it seems Mr. Scaly isn't really a con artist, after all. He's actually telling the truth. This should come as no surprise to those who understand the symbolism attached to snakes and serpents in the ancient Near East. For one thing, they were viewed as avatars of wisdom. For another, they were thought to represent immortality — their habit of shedding their skin signified an ability to regenerate and start a new life. Wisdom and immortality. The two traits the creator had denied humanity were the same two traits exemplified by the serpent.

God isn't the hero of this story, he's a repressive tyrant. Mr. Scaly, following in the esteemed footsteps of his Greek counterpart Prometheus, is doing humanity a huge favor by providing them with access to resources being withheld by a self-described jealous god. Not just jealous, but paranoid. The creator — presumably addressing other gods — states emphatically that "the man has become as one of us, discerning good and evil. He must not therefore be allowed to stretch forth his hand and take also from the tree of life, lest he eat and live forever."

The man has *become* as one of us.

Hold it right there. We've established that the humans were created in God's image, so how could they *become* like him? Moreover, if they didn't know the difference between good and evil, how could they be expected to realize that disobeying God's command was "evil" in the first place? On top of that, the woman wasn't even *alive* when God issued the command. It was directed solely at the man, so how could she be bound by it?

There are so many internal contradictions in this account that it's impossible to salvage any coherent message — at least if it's taken literally. If viewed metaphorically as a coming-of-age allegory, on the other hand, it suddenly comes into focus. The two human "children" reach the age at which they're ready to forge their own identity. They've learned to talk (naming the animals, a singular feat before the advent of See 'N Say talking toys … "the cow goes 'mooooo.' "). They've learned to do chores, tending their little garden. And they've acquainted themselves with the opposite sex. Now they're ready to choose their own clothes, rebel against their parent figure and decide to sort things out for themselves. There's an undercurrent of sexual exploration, here, too: The pair find out they're naked, and there's a sense of seduction in Eve's temptation of Adam.

An interesting aside: The name Eve is rendered in Aramaic as Hawwa, which is strikingly similar to the word for serpent — hwah. Is it the serpent seducing Adam or the woman? Or perhaps an editor merely became confused in deciphering the language of the original text and introduced Mr. Scaly (Mrs. Scaly?) into the narrative as a result. When it comes right down to it, the serpent's presence is altogether superfluous. Ancient cultures viewed sexual intercourse as a means of obtaining wisdom and maturity — the story of Enkidu in the Epic of Gilgamesh being a prime example. (In that particular tale, incidentally, Gilgamesh and Enkidu battle an adversary named Hawawa.)

Throughout ancient literature — including the Bible — wisdom is repeatedly characterized as feminine.

If we assume Mr. Scaly's presence is a result of a mistranslation and view the entire story allegorically, we have a fairly straightforward fable that illustrates the kind of tensions that can occur in a household with teenagers. Kids rebel, Dad gets huffy, hormones rage, etc. Father says, "Not under my roof!" Kids vow to strike out on their own, only to find that the world's a whole lot harsher than they could have imagined. None of this makes any sense if we take everything literally — if we make God out to be some kind of overbearing father figure who makes impossible demands and throws temper tantrums worthy of The Incredible Hulk when the kids don't live up to his expectations.

This absurd literalism, however, is exactly the means by which this fable is typically interpreted. A literal six-day creation. A snake who actually talks — presumably with forked tongue. Two magical fruit-bearing trees. Celestial beings with flaming swords that might have looked a little like the Qualta Blade wielded by Ka D'Argo in *Farscape* (obscure reference, but fans will understand it).

And creationists say the idea of evolution strains credulity? Compared to this scene worthy of a Salvador Dali painting, the idea that humans evolved from apelike creatures is an exercise in pure realism.

The hilarious byproduct of all this misrepresentation is the likelihood that our friend Mr. Scaly is the product of a simple error in translation. He probably didn't even play a part in the original story, yet he has been demonized over the centuries as the personification of evil and confused with the a figure known as "the devil." A lot of people contend the devil doesn't exist. As it turns out, he probably never did.

"There's a sucker born every minute."

— attributed to P.T. Barnum

Seven: Playing the Odds

"Why do you call me good?" Jesus once asked a man who addressed him thus. "No one is good, save God alone."

This famously ambiguous statement has fanned the flames of controversy for nearly two thousand years. What, exactly, did Jesus mean? On the face of it, he seems to have been issuing a rebuke: Don't equate me with God. I can't live up to that standard. But his words could also be taken as a way of suggesting that the other fellow had a valid reason for labeling him "good" — and identifying that reason. The unspoken implication is that the man spoke to Jesus in this manner precisely *because* he (Jesus) was, in fact, God.

It's easy to get caught up in the debate of how to interpret Jesus' meaning … without ever bothering to question his premise.

No one is good, save God alone.

Calling God "good" raises all sorts of problems. First of all, it's largely a matter of perspective. What was good for the Hebrews was a death sentence for the Canaanites displaced by the invading sons of Abraham. What was good for King David was bad news for Goliath. And so forth. According to Christians, it's "good news" (the literal meaning of the word "gospel") that Jesus died a tortured death for a crime he didn't commit — setting himself up as a king and thus committing treason against the Roman Empire.

This is supposedly the same god who declared through the prophet Hosea, "I desire mercy, not a sacrifice." Yet here he is, demanding the exact opposite— withholding mercy from Jesus and demanding that he *become* a human sacrifice. Certainly an omnipotent god would have found another way to proceed here. The way things turned out, as described in orthodox Christian theology, he manages to come off looking cruel, hypocritical and weak. Cruel because he asks that Jesus submit himself to an agonizing death. Hypocritical, because he has apparently changed his mind about valuing mercy above sacrifice. And weak because, if he's omnipotent, he could presumably come up with a different option that both spares Jesus and salvages his own reputation as a truth-teller.

If anything, this makes even less sense than hardening the pharaoh's heart. But then, the ways of god are not the ways of man … you know the routine. When the word "good" is defined as "whatever God decides to do" (or whatever people decide to do in his name), it's pretty hard to argue with the outcome. Just ask Job. Or the apostle Paul, who had the audacity to say, "Let God be proven true, and every man a liar!" Why is this so audacious? Because Paul was talking about *his* particular god and his own version of the truth. Any doubts about this can be allayed by a quick check of his letter to the Galatians — the earliest of his epistles and one that most scholars agree is probably genuine. In it, Paul places a curse on anyone who might dare to "preach a different gospel than the one we delivered to you." Even if the messenger in question is an angel.

That, my friends, is one hell of an ego.

Here we see the tribal god of the Old Testament in all his wrathful glory, insinuating himself into the New Testament narrative. He has bound and gagged his nemesis, the all-powerful supreme creator who doesn't take sides, and disguised himself in an attempt to take his place. So relentless is the tribal god in pursuing this singular goal that even Jesus — often presented as a model of tolerance and forgiveness — appears unsure about which of these two divine visions to claim as his own. In one place, he warns his followers that "those who live by the sword shall die by the sword"; yet later, he counsels them to sell their cloaks in order to buy just this sort of weapon. In one instance, he counsels them to love their enemies and turn the other cheek. Yet this same man supposedly demanded that they forsake their families to follow him, declaring that "he who is not for me is against me."

The contradictions are signs of the continual tension between the universal god and the limited god of a specific chosen people. Trying to reconcile these two ultimately irreconcilable visions, Jesus — or the authors of his life story — bounced back and forth like a pinball from one extreme to the other, at times looking just as self-contradictory as the Old Testament god of Israel. As we have seen, the latter vision ultimately won the day, consigning the Gnostic god of illumination to oblivion.

The god of today's orthodox Christian isn't the epitome of enlightenment — the creator of all things, both "good" and "evil." He's the god who takes sides with the same rabid zeal that launches crusades, violent jihads and inquisitions. This is a god who demands unflinching obedience, condemning heretics and unbelievers because he simply cannot tolerate unrighteousness. Cannot. Here we are clearly in the province of a limited god, not a limitless creator. The word "cannot" simply isn't in an almighty being's vocabulary (otherwise, he wouldn't be almighty).

The triumph of the tribal god isn't that hard to understand. In a complex and uncertain world, people crave answers. They don't want more questions. Science tells them, "We'll give you the best answer we can based on the information we have, but we can't guarantee anything. If we discover something that expands upon or contradicts what we already know, we'll have to change our conclusion."

Nor particularly reassuring.

Compare that to the claim of so-called faith: "Look no further! We *have* the answer! We *guarantee* you it's the truth, and it's never going to change. It's the same yesterday, today and forever. You can count on it!"

Now that's the sort of answer we're looking for. You'd never hear that sort of thing from a reputable scientist or a college professor. It sounds like something a carnival barker or a snake oil salesman would say — someone who has an agenda and wants to sell you something. The price? Your eternal soul. As they say, let the buyer beware. You pay your money and you take your chances.

Pascal's Wager

To hear the 17th century philosopher Blaise Pascal tell it, you've really got nothing to lose. According to a little piece of hokum known as Pascal's Wager, you're forced to place a bet on the existence of God. You're not told what sort of god, but it's assumed we're talking about the Christian deity. Pascal compares it to a celestial coin toss. If bet on God's existence and win, you break the bank; you win the jackpot. Step right up! Everyone's a winnah!!!!

But Pascal's entire argument is based on a key assumption: By comparing his wager to a coin toss, he creates the impression that winning and losing are equal possibilities. That, however, is simply not so. If the object of his wager were something as impersonal as a creative force, that might be worth a friendly game of chance. But he's arguing for a very specific sort of God: one who rewards those who bet in his favor. Once he introduces this element into the equation, the odds plummet faster than a pelican diving into the ocean to procure a fish. The moment he introduces this element into the equation, his "wager" no longer concerns the existence of God, but the *nature* of God.

Sure, God might reward people who believe in him. But he also might prefer people who keep his commandments. (This is the old faith vs. works debate that put the holy apostles Paul and James at each other's throats — if you don't believe me, read Paul's tirade against James' followers in his letter to the Galatians.) And that's just one possibility. He might prefer people of a certain skin color. Or people with a certain ethnic background. Or evangelicals, Catholics, Muslims, Mormons, etc. Heck, he might even prefer fans of the Los Angeles Angels or New Orleans Saints. The possibilities are literally endless.

So, instead of a 50-50 shot at winning, your odds tend to hover uncomfortably close to zero. Closer to winning the Powerball lottery than a coin toss. And do you really have nothing to lose? Hardly. Gods who set aside for themselves a "chosen" people routinely require members of this elect group to engage in certain activities that set them apart. Circumcision is a prime example. You're supposed to lop off a portion of your penis, which God supposedly put there in the first place, to identify the fact that you belong to him. This sort of mutilation resembles nothing more closely than a cattle brand.

Alternatively (or in addition), you may be required to engage in other forms of pointless self-denial, abstaining from sex, caffeine, alcohol, dancing, Beatles records and so forth. Please notice I referred to *pointless* self-denial. Abstaining from certain activities to improve one's health or promote discipline is all well and good. But if Pascal's wager turns out to be false — and the odds are stacked pretty hard against it — all this pious behavior will be entirely pointless. It certainly was for Job. Yet despite this, Pascal's badly flawed argument has survived for more than three-and-a-half centuries as a mainstay of Christian apologetics. The continued reliance upon such flimsy reasoning could well indicate a lack of something more substantial in the way of an argument. Millions of people wager their hard-earned money on lottery games every year, despite the astronomical odds against them. It's not the odds they're focused on, it's the jackpot.

That's why this modern variation on Pascal's wager is still attracting so many people today. They ignore the odds and keep their attention on the payoff. They have *faith* that it will occur. Of course, this doesn't change the odds, and they're nearly always disappointed. But that doesn't stop them from trying again the next time. And the next time. This phenomenon explains why people ignore the 100 percent historical failure of apocalyptic cults and repeatedly fall for claims that the end of the world is about to occur.

The most recent example of this is the billboard campaign of 2011 that promised Jesus would return on May 21 of that year. When the second coming failed to materialize as promised on this date, the man behind this prediction — a certain Harold Camping — pushed the date back to Oct. 21. He retired from his ministry just five days before this second date, and ultimately admitted he had been wrong in attempting to pin things down. In the years leading up to that not-so-fateful date, however, he had collected plenty of money from followers interested in helping him promote his message.

Camping's admission of failure, however, seems to be the exception rather than the rule. The Watchtower Society, for example, predicted the end of the world more than half a dozen times during the 20th century, starting in 1914. For 1975, it based its prediction on "reliable Bible chronology that Adam was created in the year 4026 BCE, likely in the autumn of that year, at the end of the sixth day of creation." Those pesky fossils and carbon dating results might help explain why they were off the mark on that one.

But such predictions aren't limited to fringe groups and cults. Within the Christian tradition, they can be traced back to no less a figure than Jesus himself, who plainly stated, "Some who are standing here shall not taste death until they see the son of man coming in his kingdom" (Matt 16:28). When this failed to happen, it should have been the end of the movement, but the exact opposite occurred: the movement continued to grow and became the official religion of the Roman Empire long after everyone who had heard Jesus' false prophecy was dead.

Instead of turning away from Jesus, they doubled down on their wager, creating various highly dubious scenarios in an attempt to salvage his reputation — and their own faith. One of the strangest of these was the story of the Wandering Jew, an individual who supposedly taunted Jesus on his way to be crucified and was cursed to walk the earth until the second coming. This was a handy piece of fiction on two counts: First, it served as a warning about what might happen to those who questioned Jesus; second, it "explained" that Jesus had told the truth about someone remaining alive long enough to witness his return.

The location of this Wandering Jew is, of course, never revealed. As a result, it can never be confirmed or denied, so it remains firmly in the realm of faith — an outlandish claim created to buttress the equally dubious contention that a dead man will someday return to judge the world. Oh, what a tangled web we weave …

That's faith for you. It offers an illusion of certainty that science is simply too honest to provide.

Which is exactly why it works. In the end, it's not the object of faith itself that makes the difference in one's level of certainty — it's the faith itself. I can be equally sure about the law of gravity, Jesus' resurrection and the existence of the Loch Ness Monster. Without that messy little detail called evidence to trip me up, my faith can be equally strong concerning any of these things. It doesn't matter that science has produced empirical evidence for the law of gravity time and again, while it has failed to confirm either of the other two claims.

Without worrying about evidence, we can be certain about anything. Whether it happens to be true or not, it's still absolute. That's the important thing.

"There is no such source of error as the pursuit of absolute truth."
— Samuel Butler

Eight: Absolute Values

Followers of tribal gods imagine they live in a world of absolutes. Theirs is a black and white existence devoid of nuance or gradation, where everything happens at the margins. It's either good or evil, heaven or hell, sin or righteousness, blessing or curse. There's nothing in between. Should you dare suggest that the world is far more varied and complex than this two-dimensional construct, you'll be viewed with suspicion at best, outright condemnation at worst. You'll leave yourself open to charges of employing "situational ethics" or "moral relativism" — merely for pointing out that one-size-fits-all solutions don't really fit all sizes at all. To use an analogy employed by Jesus, it's folly to put new wine into old wineskins. The skins will end up bursting, and the wine will be wasted. A more ringing endorsement of situational ethics would be hard to find, yet moral absolutists will have none of it.

Situational ethics, you see, is a concept too close to science. If the answers change according to the situation, it's a direct challenge to faith — and the tribal god's authority. He demands that his followers obey him *regardless* of the situation. Your actions aren't supposed to be dictated by the shifting sands of a fluid environment, but by the unchanging, immutable word of God. If he says the world is flat, it's flat. If he says birth control is wrong, it's wrong. If he says eating pork is a sacrilege, well, you'd better not fry that bacon.

The Torah is littered with examples of such ritual taboos. Indeed, the first five books of the Bible use the term "unclean" or some variation thereof no fewer than 140 times. It's applied to everything from dietary choices to menstruation to skin conditions.

Jesus, to his credit, apparently had little regard for such taboos. Had he worried about keeping them, he would have quickly recoiled when a woman with "an issue of blood" reached out to touch the hem of his garment. According to Leviticus, coming into contact with such a person would have rendered Jesus unclean until evening. Then there was the business of associating with similarly "unclean" individuals with a particularly nasty skin condition known as leprosy. Jesus disregarded this particular taboo more than once.

Some taboos never made much sense to begin with. The example of segregating a man for having a nocturnal emission (of semen) comes to mind. Others may have made sense at the time but have long since outlived their relevance.

Sure, God supposedly told the Israelites to refrain from eating pork. But that was during an era before meat could be preserved by modern refrigeration methods. Today's pork is much leaner than it was even a few decades ago, and it's perfectly safe to eat as long as it's cooked to 160 degrees Fahrenheit. None of this knowledge was available to the ancient Israelites, who merely noted that pigs were inclined to wallow in the mud and that their meat — improperly prepared — could cause serious illnesses. Nevertheless, some religious traditions still avoid pork on the basis that it is somehow unclean.

Even worse is the Catholic Church's objection to contraception on the ground that it violates God's supposed command to Adam and Eve: "Be fruitful and multiply; fill the Earth and subdue it." Ask anyone in Dhaka or Lagos or Mumbai whether the Earth is full, and you're liable to get the same answer. The command has been fulfilled.

Certainly no sane god would have issued such a command to *two* people and intended it to apply to 7 billion others uncounted generations later. Would he?

The pope seems to think so.

Changing circumstances don't matter, the Bible does. And the Bible doesn't change. The church is vehemently against abortion, and contraception can prevent unwanted pregnancies. Condoms, for instance, can reduce the rate of pregnancy by 85 to 98 percent. Some of those pregnancies, presumably, would end in abortion. When used properly, condoms also dramatically reduce the chances of contracting an STD. But none of this matters to a church that insists on following an obsolete commandment issued to two people long dead (if they ever even existed in the first place). Is the Catholic Church complicit in abortion? In the AIDS epidemic? I'll leave it to the reader to answer those questions.

Obsoletes and absolutes are the stock in trade of religions that place their faith in an "unchanging" god while faced with the reality of an ever-changing world. There's a good reason so many fundamentalist Christians are afraid of evolution, and it goes far beyond the appalling suggestion that humans might be descended from, in the words of Charlton Heston, a "damned dirty ape." Evolution strikes at the heart of the Christian faith in an infallible, unchanging creator. To quote the late Carl Sagan, "The fossil record implies trial and error, the inability to anticipate the future, features inconsistent with a Great Designer (though not a Designer of more remote and indirect temperament)." Simply put, evolution shatters the fundamentalist's belief in an orderly and unchanging world. It's the most damning piece of evidence in an open-and-shut case against the tribal god of wrath and vengeance. At its core is a simple principle: adapt or perish.

An unchanging god can't adapt, so his future is bleak indeed. Zeus can testify to that, as can Lugh, Inanna and a host of other gods whose names and legacies have been consigned to irrelevance or oblivion for one simple reason: They couldn't adapt to a changing world. They couldn't cut the mustard. Amen-Ra once reigned supreme in Egypt, only to be cast down from his throne by Serapis, who in turn was supplanted by Jesus, who a few centuries later succumbed to Allah. Eternal gods don't last an eternity; rather, they stick around just so long as they're relevant, then fade into the recesses of history when some new god — or more likely, his armies — proves to be more, well, adaptable.

The Squeaky Wheel

It's been said that the squeaky wheel gets the grease. In the case of religion, the loudest voice gets the greased palm. There's a reason why preachers *preach*, rather than holding roundtable discussions or seminars at universities. The voice of conviction carries the furthest, drowning out the unspoken doubts that gnaw at the back of one's cranium by cranking up the levels of both the volume and the braggadocio to 10 and beyond.

Those who lack faith gravitate toward those who *appear* to exude it.

This is why the bulk of Christian theology does not stem from the church's putative founder, Jesus, who vowed that the meek would inherit the earth. Instead it can be traced to a bombastic, self-important individual who many conclude never even met the man but had the temerity to hijack his movement and appoint himself its leader. This was none other than the so-called "apostle" Paul, who wrote seven books of the New Testament (his authorship of six others is disputed), compared to not a single word from Jesus himself.

Paul was not an apostle. Jesus did not appoint him as one of the original twelve, and when a position opened up among this number, he was not the one selected to fill it. He was a Roman Jew from Tarsus who had no particular love for Jesus' original inner circle or the man who succeeded Jesus as its leader — his brother, James. In his letter to the Galatians, he refused to recognize James' authority and boasted that he opposed his representative, Cephas (Peter), "to his face because he stood condemned."

Paul seemed to like boasting. He did quite a lot of it in his second letter to Corinth, which he claims to be "not in the least inferior to those super-apostles" and goes on at great length seeking to establish himself as an apostle. One gets the impression of a man very much on the defensive, and with a very high opinion of himself. Remember, this is the man who told his followers to spurn anyone who dared to contradict him — even an angel.

Now *that's* self-confidence. Call it faith, or arrogance, if you prefer. But however you label it, this particular quality works like a charm in attracting people who lack it. "I'm not really sure what to believe, but this person seems so sure of himself, he *must* know something." So the line of reasoning goes. In reality, however, the "something" he knows is how to work a crowd, make a sale and close a deal.

The more self-assured a person appears, the more easily he can persuade others accept what he has to say. In essence, he becomes their surrogate in the faith game. They don't have enough of it, so he generously provides it with his confident demeanor and "guaranteed results." A tireless promoter can sell virtually anything, no matter how incredible.

It's no accident that Paul himself was the most vocal advocate of the faith movement he hijacked from Jesus. He developed a vast network of followers throughout the Levant and Asia Minor, then ensured their loyalty by alternately goading, encouraging and berating them in a series of letters designed to ensure their continued allegiance. His knack for self-promotion not only paid personal dividends, it paved the way for his ideas to eclipse those of Jesus as the basis for a belief system that would convert billions.

Paul was certainly not the only preacher to use arrogance and charisma as a recipe for winning over the masses — qualities he augmented with a not-so-subtle curse against anyone who might "preach a gospel other than the one we preached to you." Threats are another way to convey certainty, because they imply the person making them has the means to back them up. Sure, it's always possible that the threat is nothing more than a bluff, but the better the bully's poker face, the less inclined you'll be to call it. And the more cocksure your opponent is, the more likely you are to fold. It's better to be on the winning side, after all, than to risk all hell breaking loose if you decide to up the ante.

The Corbomite Maneuver

One of my all-time favorite television moments occurs in an episode of Star Trek titled *The Corbomite Maneuver*. The third episode ever filmed, it's the first to feature the character of Dr. McCoy. In it, the starship Enterprise stumbles into a region of space claimed by an ominous looking alien named Balok. This dour-faced character summarily passes judgment against the crew of the Enterprise for trespassing and destroying a space buoy, giving them ten minutes to pray to their deities before their ship is destroyed. Apparently outgunned and without any means of defending themselves, Captain Kirk and Co. appear to be doomed. Even Mr. Spock, the science officer, gives them no hope for survival, declaring that "in chess, when one player is outmatched, the game is over — checkmate."

This, he says, is the only logical conclusion.

After a few tense moments mulling the situation, however, Kirk hits on an alternative: "Not chess," he tells Spock. "Poker."

He then contacts the alien vessel and informs Balok that the Enterprise is carrying a material known as corbomite — a substance of such power that it would obliterate any ship foolish enough to launch an attack. In actuality, there's no such thing. The bluff works, however, and Kirk is subsequently invited aboard Balok's ship … only to find that the menacing-looking Balok himself is an illusion, and the "man behind the curtain" is really a childlike alien played by Ron Howard's younger brother, Clint. As it turns out, *both sides* were bluffing.

The key to both deceptions was the appearance of strength, exhibited in the form of confidence that incites fear, even panic, in the other party. The alien's image appears on the screen as a stoic mask of inevitability. The actual alien uses this façade in Oz-like fashion to obscure his true, far-less-threatening form, and the intimidation tactic works like a charm. At one point during the episode, a member of the Enterprise crew becomes hysterical at the prospect of the ship's apparently imminent destruction. The tension created on the bridge of ship is palpable, and even Kirk himself appears on the verge of cracking.

Once he figures out how to fight the alien, however, Kirk, for his part, exhibits supreme confidence in the ability of the imaginary corbomite to blow his adversary out of the sky. Each side is literally playing god, claiming to hold the power of life and death over the other. The result, on both ends, is fear … and faith — not faith in the sense that we often think of it, but faith nonetheless. Faith in a false construct designed to fool one's target audience.

It's the same sort of faith inspired by such phrases as "fear of the lord is the beginning of wisdom."

This is one reason negative political campaigns work so well, and why preachers repeatedly resort to hellfire-and-brimstone sermons to rouse their congregations. Scare tactics work in real life as well as they do in poker. Fear, imparted from behind a veneer of confidence, creates faith — in the messenger.

Or the preacher.

The faith isn't really in "God," but rather, in *the preacher's vision* of God. It isn't a personal faith, but a faith by proxy. It's not hard to recognize the vast potential for abuse inherent in such a situation. As Lord Acton famously warned, "Power tends to corrupt, and absolute power corrupts absolutely" — and power doesn't get much more absolute than the sort wielded by a supreme, omnipotent creator.

As we have seen, however, the existence of such a god is far from self-evident. Our senses tell us that the tree in the front yard exists, but they offer no such comparable evidence for the divine.

The preacher, however, does.

Or claims to.

In making such a claim, he sets himself up as the voice of God on Earth. Suddenly, a fallible human dares to assert that he speaks for an infallible God. The Old Testament prophets did it. Jesus did it, too. He told his followers he could do only what he saw the Father doing. Translation: If you question me, you question God himself. Once Jesus was dead, this divine authority supposedly transferred to Peter (the man Paul personally "condemned") and his successors in Rome; the supposedly infallible pope claims it to this very day. The Islamic shahada, or creed, hints at the same sort of principle: "There is no god but Allah, and Muhammad is his prophet." No pope or prophet would be necessary if God could speak clearly and unequivocally on his own behalf, but the days of burning bushes and voices from heaven appear to be over. Because God can't, or won't speak for himself — or perhaps because he doesn't exist — others are left to do the dirty work for him.

Or to fashion him out of corbomite.

All this would be well and good if the humans who claimed to speak on his behalf were actually a) infallible and b) incorruptible, but the history of the papacy makes it quite clear that the Roman pontiff is neither.

Martin Luther finally became fed up with all this silliness when he declared that God had no need of a middleman to conduct witch hunts, sell indulgences and keep the masses ignorant. He therefore came up with a concept called the "priesthood of all believers," which dispensed with such priestly power plays as confession, penance and the right to preside over — or withhold — the sacraments. This would seem to have been a great leap forward, but it addressed the symptom rather than the cause. While many Christians felt the priesthood was hopelessly corrupt and onerous (as it clearly was), they also lacked either the will or the capacity to figure God out for themselves. Many were illiterate, and those educated enough to make their own judgments came to vastly different conclusions about the nature of God.

It all got very messy.

The "solution" was to replace priestly authority with biblical authority, but this was really no solution at all. Those who couldn't read were out of luck, and this was still a large percentage of the population. Three years before the dawn of the 20th century, only 28 percent of Russians were literate. In 1841, more one-third of Englishmen and nearly half of Englishwomen "signed" their marriage certificates with a simple mark because they didn't know how to write. This was more than three centuries *after* Luther nailed his famed 95 theses to the Wittenberg Door.

Absent the ability to read, the masses still needed someone to tell them what the Bible said. Into this yawning chasm stepped the pastor or preacher, who was only too glad to take up the mantle of the defrocked priesthood in Protestant lands. As more people learned to read, literacy became less of an impediment, but this development did nothing to address the root issue: People wracked by uncertainty gravitate to those who appear self-confident, putting their faith in such surrogates because they look like they know what they're doing. The contradictions in the Bible itself don't help, and it's only natural that laymen should turn to self-appointed experts to sort out all the troubling inconsistencies (under the dubious assumption that they can be sorted out at all).

This is just the first step of the process. Once they commit themselves, these followers are asked to invest more and more of their time, energy and money in the cause identified by the surrogate as "God's will." This solidifies the surrogate's hold on his flock. The more of your time, energy and the more of *yourself* you invest in something, the less willing you'll be to re-examine it. You don't want to pour your heart and soul into a belief system, only to find out — again, in Jesus' words — that you've built your house upon the sand. That's why people will defend the indefensible with their very lives. It has nothing at all to do with reason or common sense; it has everything to do with protecting their investment, whether that investment is emotional, temporal or monetary.

If you've believed something for 20 years, it's difficult to change at the drop of a hat.

"Knowledge makes a man unfit to be a slave."

— Frederick Douglass

Nine: Drink the Kool-Aid

In a sense, we're all slaves — not to some God out there, but to our own fears and emotions.

Once we've bought into the poker game of faith, the stakes grow higher with every chip we throw into the pot. The further the game progresses, the more we have to lose.

This may help explain a phenomenon known as Stockholm syndrome, a term used to describe the behavior of hostages who develop sympathy for — and loyalty to — their abductors. This doesn't happen right away. The captors typically threaten their victims with dire consequences should they try to escape, providing food and shelter but not the slightest semblance of freedom. After a time, a particular kind of defense mechanism starts to kick in. Unable to escape, they resign themselves to their plight and seek to preserve what little they can count on: the security provided by their captors. In order to do so, however, they must repress their own shame at being unable to escape. This is accomplished by rationalizing their situation. "It's not really as bad as it seems … I actually kind of like it here. Why should I *want* to escape?" After a time, the victim comes to view his or her captor as a sort of benefactor.

Perhaps the best-known example of this was the abduction of newspaper heiress Patricia Hearst by a radical group known as the Symbionese Liberation Army. Hearst, who was 19 at the time, came to accept the group's mission as her own, joining its ranks, changing her name to "Tania" and ultimately even participating in a bank robbery. She was arrested and ultimately served 22 months in prison.

Her reaction is hardly uncommon. Victims of domestic abuse often rationalize staying with their abusive partners and even wind up defending them from the threat of arrest or prosecution. Abusers — whether they are kidnappers or perpetrators of domestic terror — tend to isolate their victims for a reason. Their goal is to establish a "new normal" without allowing anyone on the outside to challenge it. By continually reinforcing the false reality they have created, these monsters gradually break down their victims' defenses until those victims buy into the illusion. It's a classic and effective strategy. The kidnapper removes the victim's safety net and replaces it … with himself. He becomes the best friend, parent, counselor, even God. And there's nowhere else to turn.

This was the strategy followed in the 1800s by a man named Joseph Smith, who founded an organization called The Church of Jesus Christ of Latter-day Saints. Try saying that three times real fast. It was also followed, with even more dire consequences, by a man named Jim Jones more than a century later.

We'll deal with Joseph Smith first.

Lost Tribes and Buried Treasure

The religion he founded, commonly known as Mormonism, claims more than 13 million baptized followers worldwide.

Critical thinkers have a big advantage in dealing with the claims of Mormonism that they lack when looking at many other religions. The claims made by Joseph Smith were made relatively recently, so they're easier to check. The founders of other religious traditions (Moses, the Buddha, Jesus and Muhammad, for example) are shadowy figures who lived more than one, two or three thousand years ago. Their methods and motives have been passed down to us second- or third-hand through their followers. Many details of their lives are lost to us.

The founder of Mormonism, by contrast, lived less than two centuries ago. His belief system was forged under the microscope of modern scrutiny. We may know virtually nothing about the first thirty years of Jesus' life, for example, but we know the details of Joseph Smith's life in detail. We know, for instance, that Smith's "profession" before he founded the Mormon church was (are you ready?) looking for buried treasure, using a stone with a hole in it.

It never worked. We know it didn't work. Yet Smith employed a variation on this method in "translating" the Book of Mormon from a set of tablets that no one else ever saw. He literally dictated the contents from behind a curtain, serving as a sort of precursor to L. Frank Baum's not-so-wonderful wizard.

At least, it some might suggest, he had turned his attention from a quest for personal enrichment to more spiritual matters. Unfortunately, this was not the case. Before long, Smith set about using his fledgling faith as the basis for a get-rich-quick scheme that involved setting up a bank for the Mormon community. When the bank (known as the Kirtland Safety Society) failed, many members of the church were left bankrupt and Smith himself was fined for running an illegal operation.

Smith had far less in common with Jesus than he did with Donald Trump or his own contemporary P.T. Barnum. He lived in an era before government regulation was in place to curtail this nefarious sort of free enterprise. Snake-oil salesmen, con men and charlatans were a dime a dozen. Part of what set Smith apart is that he was able to produce a new collection of "scripture" that purported to reveal a connection between ancient Judeo-Christian tradition and the Americas.

In a young nation working to establish its identity, this was a master stroke. Except the "new" scripture really wasn't new at all.

Some sections were apparently borrowed from an 1825 book The *Wonders of Nature* by Josiah Priest. And approximately 2,000 words were taken from the New Testament, while 25,000 others were drawn from the Old — most of them via a book called *View of the Hebrews* by Ethan Smith, published just seven years before The Book of Mormon.

Ethan Smith's book postulated that Native Americans had colonized the New World from the Middle East, a hypothesis taken up by Joseph Smith. (The two Smiths were no relation.)

Unfortunately for Joseph Smith and those who put their faith in him, this turned out to be a bunch of hogwash. Genetic tests have shown that Native Americans originated in Central Asia, precisely the opposite direction of the Middle East. They migrated to the Americas, at the latest, some 16,000 years ago — not 2,600 years ago as Smith's writings suggest. One can state conclusively that Native Americans did not come from the Middle East, because we know they came from somewhere else entirely.

Smith seems to have encountered opposition nearly everywhere he went. He led his followers across the country, from New York to Ohio to Missouri and, finally, Illinois. He was ultimately arrested for treason against the state of Illinois and was killed when an angry mob broke into the jail where he was held and shot him. His successor, Brigham Young, subsequently moved farther west and founded the Utah territory as a haven for Mormonism.

Jonestown

This brings us to the case of the megalomaniacal preacher Jim Jones, who followed a similar pattern in relocating his "flock" from Indiana to San Francisco and, ultimately, to Guyana in South America — no doubt hoping to emulate Young and set up a sort of insulated Shangri-La where his unconventional belief system could flourish without any outside interference.

It was in the 1970s that Jones whisked nearly 1,000 people away from their homes in California to the tiny Third World nation.

In doing so, he created a literally captive audience and a situation that was ripe for abuse.

Isolated and cut off from family and friends back home, those who followed Jones to his South American "sanctuary" had nowhere else to turn but to the man responsible for their predicament. But unlike Young, Jones lived in a world of air travel and television news; no matter how far he traveled, he couldn't completely segregate his followers from the "outside world."

It wasn't long before a team of government officials, who had been contacted by concerned relatives, came to investigate. The visitors were allowed to speak with the members of Jones' commune, most of whom defended their leader vehemently. But a few members of the community (called Jonestown after Jones) expressed a desire to leave. Jones did nothing at first to impede them. But when the delegation had left the encampment, he had his thugs follow them and open fire as the group prepared to board a small, twin-engine plane.

U.S. Rep. Leo Ryan and four others were killed in the assault.

The shootings were meant to serve two purposes. First, they would keep Ryan from revealing any negative information about Jonestown to the outside world. Second, they would reinforce the fear among those who remained behind by illustrating, in the most graphic terms possible, what would happen to anyone who dared to betray their leader. Such extreme measures, however, only brought the entire project crashing down on their heads. Jones, realizing he couldn't escape from the backlash that was sure to follow, instructed his followers to drink fruit punch (not actually Kool-Aid, despite the pop culture references) laced with cyanide. They willingly did so. In all, 909 people died that day in 1978.

What makes the entire incident even more chilling is that Jones' strategy of isolating his followers from the people who cared most about them — their families — was the same strategy reportedly employed by another messianic figure.

Jesus.

When a certain young man approached him and asked how he might inherit eternal life, Jesus told him he should "sell everything, then give the money to the poor and you shall have treasure in heaven; then come and follow me." This is exactly the sort of strategy employed by abusive spouses, kidnappers and delusional characters like Jim Jones: attempt to isolate your target, remove his safety net and render him utterly dependent upon … you.

Jesus' particular injunction in this case is rendered all the more suspect when one realizes that his followers often referred to themselves as Ebionites — a word that means "the poor." It's quite possible that Jesus was telling the young man to give his money to "the cause," in much the same way televangelists beg their viewers for money every Sunday.

Another speech attributed to Jesus advocates a similar approach and is, if anything, even more disturbing. In a lengthy address to his inner circle, he lectures them about the importance of loyalty. "Do not suppose," he tells them, "that I have come to bring peace upon the earth. I came not to bring peace, but a sword. I have come to turn a man against his father and a daughter upon her mother; a daughter-in-law against her mother-in-law, that a man's enemies shall be the members of his own household." Indeed, he continued, "anyone who loves his father or mother more than me is unworthy of me; anyone who loves son or daughter more is unworthy of me" (Matt. 10:34-37).

Here again, Jesus has shrugged off the supreme god of inclusion and is preaching the "gospel" of the tribal god — the god who takes sides in no uncertain terms. "Whoever acknowledges me before others, I will acknowledge before my heavenly father," he declares. "And whoever disowns me before others, I will likewise disown before my heavenly father." This sounds a lot more like an eye for an eye than the dictum Jesus supposedly coined to supplant it: turn the other cheek. Then again, maybe God expects a higher standard of his followers than he's willing to follow himself.

Be that as it may, he's asking that his followers be ready to repudiate their families and put all their faith in him: the Jim Jones strategy.

In Jesus' defense, there's no indication in the Bible that he ever took advantage of the situation to abuse his followers directly. However, it should also be noted that the four gospels are hardly unbiased works, and one wouldn't expect them to contain accounts of Jesus mistreating his disciples. The point is not, ultimately, to condemn Jesus himself but rather to point out that his words have "inspired" numerous modern followers who have no problem isolating and abusing others for the sake of the so-called good news. Among the most hard-core fundamentalists, outside influences are shunned for fear that they might be "of the devil." Quoting the first canonical epistle attributed to Peter, they warn, "Your adversary, the devil, prowls about like a roaring lion, seeking whom he might devour" (1 Pet. 5:8). Worse yet, according to Paul, he often takes the form of an "angel of light."

This level of paranoia makes one feel sorry for those *genuine* angels of light who get mistaken for some demonic imposter.

But it's better to condemn a few innocents than to let the guilty avoid punishment, right?

That's the rationale.

What it leads to is a sort of spiritual quarantine. Believers are not allowed to engage in any or all of the following activities: dancing, listening to popular music, drinking caffeine or using contraception. They are to refrain from working on the Sabbath or exposing themselves to anything identified as "secular." This includes certain movies, theater productions and types of music. It also most definitely includes lectures concerning evolution and sexuality — especially *homo*sexuality. Better to bury your head in the sand than to risk being deceived or corrupted. To hear some people talk with such fear about the concept of sin, one might think they were referring to a strain of the black plague rather than an act of personal volition. And that's exactly how many folks seem to view it. They view sin as a contagion or inherited condition, one passed down from generation to generation since the dawn of humankind.

Let's get one thing straight right now. Greek is the language of the New Testament, and the Greek word most commonly translated as "sin" is *hamartia*. It means simply "to miss the mark." Sometimes, the word *anomia* is used, which refers to lawlessness. Neither of these words has anything to do with a contagious disease or something passed down in one's DNA. (Heck, the people who wrote them hadn't the faintest inkling there even *was* such a thing as DNA.) The point is that *hamartia* functions as a verb. It's something a person does.

The Greek word for disease in the New Testament is, in fact, a noun, but it isn't *anomia*. It's *noson*. I don't believe the Bible even mentions contagious diseases beyond a few specific references to leprosy.

All this may be of very little interest to the reader, but let me assure you, it's important. Virtually all the weight of Paul's theology rests on the concept of original sin, which posits that sin is in fact some sort of terminal condition. You can act in whatever manner you wish, but it makes no difference: You are still a sinner *by definition* — which is why you need Jesus to "save" you. That would make Paul's theology entirely dispensable. He couldn't allow that, so he constructed a doctrine under which it was impossible to attain any degree of moral nobility or affirm any sort of self-worth.

This is exactly how abusers act. They shame their victims into believing they're worthless, then proceed to blame them for everything. By doing so, they create a culture of dependence. The victims come to believe they are so incompetent they can't possibly make it on their own. They need their abusers, who portray themselves as benefactors … all the while demeaning, accusing and reviling their chosen targets.

Such vile behavior is justified on the ground that the supposedly beneficent abuser has "chosen" his victim, from among all the people on the face of the earth — and despite some gross and unforgivable defects — to be his own. It's an honor.

He calls it "love."

Slave Trade

Followers of Paul's theology firmly believe that they are, in the words of the famous spiritual folk tune *Amazing Grace*, "wretches" who have been saved. The sad irony is that this particular tune became a favorite of the African American community, none of whom were wretches who needed to be saved. On the contrary, they were residents of another continent who were minding their own business when they were forcibly abducted and separated from their homes, their families and everything they knew. They were then introduced to a new god, the god of their abusers, who used his "holy writ" to justify abusing them. The book of Colossians gave them license to do so when it enjoined slaves to "obey your earthly masters in all things; and do it not merely when their eyes are upon you to win their favor, but with sincerity of heart and reverence for the lord." Moreover, the dark pigment of their skin identified them as descendants of the biblical figure named Ham, one of Noah's three sons, whose supposed black skin was viewed as a sign that he was cursed.

One problem: The Bible never says anything about Ham having dark skin. This spurious detail only surfaced later, in extracanonical folklore. The passage does, however, say is that Ham brought a curse upon his line by having the misfortune of looking upon his drunken father's naked body. This makes about as much sense as blaming a pedestrian hit by someone driving under the influence. The fault in this incident as portrayed in Genesis clearly lies with Noah for getting so drunk that he lay down naked and neglected to cover himself. To compound the injustice, however, Ham isn't the one cursed as a result of this. Rather, it's his son Canaan, who is condemned to be "the lowest of slaves."

So, the innocent son of an innocent man is made to bear the

weight of a relatively mild transgression by his grandfather. Certainly Noah's drunkenness, while embarrassing, was a trivial indiscretion compared to the tragedy that can result from drunken driving. At least we can praise him for knowing enough not to get behind the wheel — or rather the stick — of his ox goad drunk.

Such is the justice dispensed by the tribal god of the Old Testament. The entire story was doubtless concocted to explain why the Canaanites, who just happened to be the Hebrews' main rival for land and power in ancient Palestine, were such nasty fellows (at least from the Hebrew perspective). A putative ancestor named Canaan was created and blamed for some past transgression as a pretext for condemning the Canaanites to slavery … and justifying the Hebrews' subjugation of them. Then, a few thousand years later, a different group of invaders used the same story to justify an equally barbaric trans-Atlantic slave trade.

Here's the kicker: Eventually, the slaves who were ripped from their homeland and their families adopted the religion of their masters.

One thing should be abundantly clear to any thinking individual: The people abducted from the African continent to serve the "needs" of white plantation owners were innocent victims of abuse. They were not evil descendants of a cursed individual who happened to see his father naked. What's perhaps even worse than all this is the fact that this very same sort of reasoning isn't applied only to a single race, but to the whole of humankind. The story of Ham, in which a single supposed transgression brings a curse down upon uncounted generations, mirrors the story of Adam, who likewise is said to have brought a curse down upon *his* descendants by committing a single act.

In neither case is the guilty party culpable. Canaan, as we have seen, was cursed for his father's unintentional breach of social etiquette. Adam, for his part, was cursed for disobeying a command to abstain from the fruit of a tree that would supposedly allow him to determine whether disobedience was wrong. Talk about a Catch-22.

No modern court of law would ever convict either man of so much as a misdemeanor. The prosecution would be laughed out of court. Yet based on these flimsy accusations, millions upon millions of men have been slaughtered, and many millions more enslaved, imprisoned, exiled and deprived of their worldly goods.

This is the legacy of the god of Job.

The American justice system is built, in part, on the presumption of innocence. But there is no such innocence in Paul's theology. Every human individual is not only presumed guilty but judged to be so without a shred of evidence. The only basis for our condemnation? The words of priests and self-proclaimed prophets who lived hundreds or thousands of years ago and wrote for a culture that has little in common with our own. They wrote, in large measure, to justify and preserve their own status and power, and their words — other than a few pearls of timeless wisdom interspersed between the blood and dogma — had nothing whatsoever to do with us.

When Isaiah said a young woman would give birth, he wasn't prophesying about a virgin, let alone one named Mary. He was speaking to Ahaz, the king of Judah, a man alive in his own day. He specifically said a young woman (not a virgin) was destined to give birth, and that her son would be named Immanuel (not Jesus). The level of revisionism needed to force this square peg of a prophecy into the round hole of the New Testament narrative opens the door to so many competing interpretations it boggles the mind. You can make the Bible — or any other document — say virtually whatever you want it to say, then claim to be speaking with the authority of Almighty God.

That's the very essence of corruption born of power. It's not pretty, it's not rational and it's certainly not loving.

Then again, victims of abuse seldom realize the extent of what's been done to them until they manage to escape. There's a sickening realization that dawns on a person the more he studies an abuser's shameful strategy. It works. It's gallingly, horrifically effective. On the small scale of a single kidnapped victim or on a massive scale that enslaves an entire race of people. One need not enter an Orwellian universe to witness the upside-down reality of abuse disguised as love. The man behind the curtain is no wizard, but a priest waiting to take our confessions for sins far less than what his mother church has committed.

Here is the cold, hard truth that is staring back at us: the image of a "loving" god who kills his own son ... so that we might earn the "privilege" of being called this poor fellow's brothers and sisters. Excuse me, but I want no part of such a hopelessly dysfunctional family, and I want nothing to do with a religion that condemns people based on their supposed nature — or the color of their skin — rather than judging them on the merits of their actions.

Who are we to judge a god? Hideous wretches held in thrall to some vile condition known as sin? Vessels of clay molded on a potter's wheel? Pawns on a chessboard? Or perhaps, just perhaps, we are sentient individuals who have every right to question an abusive religious elite that maintains power by suggesting that we, the masses, are deficient and in need of *their* guidance. They tell us they speak with the authority of an almighty god, but what evidence do they offer to support this? A book full of atrocities and contradictions that claims to be authoritative based only upon ... well ... its own authority?

Such self-promoting circular reasoning simply doesn't stand up to any kind of scrutiny. "Jesus loves me, this I know, for the Bible tells me so."

If he's really still alive, the least he could do is have the courtesy to meet me over coffee and tell me himself.

"It is better to risk saving a guilty person than to condemn an innocent."

— Voltaire

Ten: Eyewitness Testimony

Often in the gospels, Jesus' opponents approach him and seek to engage him in a rhetorical battle of wits. In almost every case, the gospel writers depict them as walking away with their collective tails between their legs. This is hardly surprising when one considers that the authors' agenda was to promote a positive image of the man they considered their savior. Still, the exchanges can be entertaining. The Pharisees, who normally act as Jesus' would-be foils in these encounters, aren't very sympathetic characters, and it can be fun to watch Jesus get the best of them. He avoids falling into their best-laid traps concerning John the Baptist's mission, taxation and the proper punishment for an adulteress.

Still, one of the most interesting exchanges in the gospels occurs when some Pharisees approach Jesus and challenge him concerning the truth of his testimony. In this case, though the author of John would never admit it, Jesus clearly comes out on the short end of the stick.

The Pharisees immediately go on the attack. "Here you are," they tell Jesus, "appearing as your own witness! Your testimony is (therefore) not valid." Their unspoken precedent is a principle elucidated in Mosaic law, that one witness is not enough to convict anyone accused of a crime. According to the Book of Deuteronomy, a matter had to be established by the testimony of three, or at the very least, two witnesses.

One might expect Jesus to respond with an objection: He wasn't being accused of a crime, so the standard set for such a court case didn't apply. It might have been an effective rejoinder, but he didn't use it.

Instead, he told his accusers, "Even if I testify on my own behalf, my testimony is valid, for I know whence I came and the place to which I am going. But you have no idea whence I came or where I go. You judge according to human standards; I pass judgment on no one. But if I do judge, my judgments are true, for I am not alone. I stand with my father who sent me. In your own law, it is written that the testimony of two witnesses is true. I testify in my own behalf, and my other witness is my father, who sent me."

The Pharisees responded by, logically enough, asking him to produce his father. But instead of doing so, Jesus declared that "if you knew me, you would know the father also."

A more convoluted, circuitous bit of reasoning is scarcely to be found anywhere. First Jesus says he passes judgment on no one. Then, in the next breath, he states a peculiar caveat: "But if I do …" Which is it? He seems to want to have things both ways. Indeed, the very statement that his opponents were judging by human standards is, in effect, an exercise in passing judgment on *their* judgment.

Confused yet? It gets worse.

Jesus first argues that he doesn't need a second witness. Then he says he has one — and even acknowledges the law that states the testimony of a second witness validates that of the first. In doing so, he has effectively backed himself into a corner, all but daring his opponents to demand that he produce the promised witness. Yet when they take the bait, he flatly refuses to do so, stating indignantly that a second witness isn't necessary, after all.

The end result is that Jesus winds up speaking on God's behalf and just asking people to take his word for it. No second witness ever steps forward, and Jesus merely offers hearsay evidence of his testimony. In doing so, he sinks to the level of so many self-appointed spokesmen (and women) for God who ask others simply to take their word for it when they intone, in a voice often lowered an octave to convey a sense of gravity, "Thus sayeth the Lord!"

My response: "Says you!"

I'm sorry, but I have to side with the Pharisees on this one. They might have been, as the gospels portray them, anal-retentive control freaks and preening narcissists, but they had a point on this one. The author of John portrays them as being confounded by Jesus' circular reasoning — or perhaps simply so confused by it they threw up their hands and said, "To hell with it!" But I find I must continue to press the issue and ask, "Can I get a witness?"

The Resurrection Runaround

The resurrection is the key event in the story of Jesus. As Paul bluntly put it, "If Christ is not risen, our preaching is for naught — and so is your faith!"

That's quite a statement. Think about it. Paul is pinning his entire theology on an event without precedent in human history and fundamentally at odds with natural cycle of birth and death. To paraphrase Christopher Hitchens, the claim that Jesus rose from the dead is an extraordinary one, to say the least, and as such requires extraordinary proof. Apparently, some of Paul's followers in Corinth had a problem accepting it, because he felt the need to set them straight. Unfortunately, he offers no substantial evidence whatsoever to support his belief.

Instead, he resorts to more circular reasoning: If there were no resurrection, his preaching and his followers' faith would be in vain. However, because we *know* that Paul's preaching is substantial and his followers' faith is meaningful (don't we?), then the *resurrection* must be true. Preaching concerning what? The resurrection. Faith in what? The resurrection. That sad fact is that, when this argument is boiled down to its essential core, it amounts to a statement that "what I believe is believable because I believe it." If this doesn't constitute an example of blind faith, I don't know what does.

Fortunately for those of us who want to hang our hats on something a little more substantial, this feeble argument failed to satisfy many of Paul's successors. Over the course of the past two millennia, Christian apologists have spent inordinate amounts of time and energy seeking to make a cogent case that Jesus did, in fact, rise from the dead. The first difficulty arises from the fact that there's absolutely no empirical evidence to suggest this ever occurred. The closest thing to it is the so-called Shroud of Turin, a linen cloth that bears what looks like be a negative photographic image of a man who appears to have suffered a violent death, perhaps by crucifixion. Unfortunately for the apologists, the shroud raises more questions than it answers.

Some of those questions have been, in fact, been addressed by studying the shroud's material. An examination of the weave used in creating the shroud found it to be inconsistent with the weave from another burial cloth unearthed in first-century Jerusalem. Of course, that's hardly conclusive. Different weaves of different sorts might have been used during the same time period (just ask devotees of disco-era polyester suits). Radiocarbon dating, however, places the shroud's origins at the earliest c. 1260 CE, with an estimated accuracy of 95 percent. This would be fully consistent with the written history of the shroud: The first clear and unquestioned reference to the shroud occurs in a bishop's memorandum dating from 1390.

Even if all this evidence were to be discredited or disregarded, we would be asked to believe that the image on the shroud was that of Jesus and that it appeared as a byproduct of his resurrection. There's not a single fiber of evidence to support either conclusion. In fact, we're being asked to *assume* the resurrection took place as a means of explaining a phenomenon that supposedly proves it! And all we have here is more circular reasoning.

Without any physical evidence to rely upon, apologists rely on the converse: an *absence* of such evidence. If no resurrection had occurred, they argue, we'd have a tomb containing a body to examine. This is the weakest sort of argument: "Since your hypothesis cannot be proven, mine must, by default, be correct." It's also yet another example of the either/or mentality that's typical of the monotheist's black-and-white thinking. Of course, there are plenty of other possibilities. Someone might have removed the body from its initial resting place for burial elsewhere. Jesus might have somehow survived the crucifixion ordeal (which, according to the gospels, lasted for a far shorter time than the typical crucifixion). The body might have been stolen. The initial information about where he was buried might have been incorrect.

There is, of course, no way to test any of these hypotheses two thousand years after the fact, any more than we can test the resurrection hypothesis. Nevertheless, as stated earlier, extraordinary claims require extraordinary levels of proof — and such proof, on an empirical level, simply is nonexistent in this case.

Absent empirical data, the Christian apologist turns to the concept discussed earlier: eyewitness testimony — which is, sad to say, "notoriously unreliable." Those aren't my words. They're the words of former U.S. Supreme Court Justice William J. Brennan Jr. According to the Innocence Project, "eyewitness misidentification is the single greatest cause of wrongful convictions nationwide, playing a role in nearly 75% of convictions overturned through DNA testing."

The project is a nonprofit legal group that advocates DNA testing as a means of re-examining questionable convictions. Its website (innocenceproject.org) states that "30 years of strong social science research has proven that eyewitness identification is often unreliable. Research shows that the human mind is not like a tape recorder; we neither record events exactly as we see them, nor recall them like a tape that has been rewound."

The problem with so-called eyewitness evidence lies in how it's gathered and preserved. Each witness will view things from a unique perspective. For instance, looking at a herd of elephants from a helicopter flying over the African savanna is a lot different than standing a few feet away from one at the San Diego Zoo. The helicopter passenger may well report that the animal looks small, while the zoo patron is likely to remark how large it is. Differing physical vantage points have created conflicting testimony in many court cases because of this simple principle, and the problems go beyond physical limitations. Witnesses have their own internal perspectives to deal with, as well. Their memories are filtered through their own experiences and biases. This is why lawyers are careful to weed out members a jury pool who they believe may be biased one way or the other.

Did the resurrection actually occur? In answering this question, we are asked to credit the verdict of four men (the gospel writers) whose motives are clearly biased in favor of the assertion that Jesus rose from the dead. These men aren't witnesses; they're advocates. Only one of the four — the author of John — even claims to have seen the events he's describing. Two others are silent on whether or not they were present. The fourth, meanwhile, admits in the introduction to his work that he's compiling information others have set down before him.

Two of the four books — Mark and Luke — are attributed to followers of Paul, not Jesus. Of the other two, much of Matthew is borrowed directly from Mark, suggesting that a supposed eyewitness relied heavily on someone *who wasn't even there*, while John has been dated to five or six decades after the events described. If the author did, in fact, witness the events he wrote about, he must have been a very old man by the time he set pen to parchment. His memory was certainly no longer fresh, but then again, he wasn't trying to write a historical account anyway. In fact, he makes no bones about his personal bias, stating in his concluding remarks that "these things are written that you may believe Jesus is the anointed one, the Son of God, that believing, you may have life in his name." The end.

Statements such as this make it almost comical that witnesses in American courtrooms are called upon to swear on the Bible as proof of their veracity. Imagine if a witness revealed that he was testifying, not to establish the facts of the matter, but rather to promote his own personal agenda. Such a witness would lose all credibility with the court and would likely be admonished by some officer of the court to "remember, you're under oath."

What about the witnesses?

In seeking to prove a case, several witnesses may see things from different perspectives. This fact is often used to explain away the variations and outright contradictions present among the gospel accounts. That explanation, however, doesn't jibe with the claim that the Bible is supposedly "inspired" — dictated from the mind of an omniscient god whose work is held up as *infallible*. You can't have it both ways. Either the Bible is altogether perfect, or it contains problems that need to be explained away.

Give the apologists credit, though. At least they recognize that inconsistencies can arise from different perspectives — even if they only pay attention to this principle when it appears to suit their purposes.

How widely do perspectives vary? They can be all over the map. Not only are we constrained by our senses' limited access to our environment, but also by our temporal, cultural and personal contexts. Take, for instance, the "worldwide" flood mentioned earlier. The context in which this was written doubtless indicates a reference to the Tigris-Euphrates floodplain. For readers in the Dark Ages, the "world" was a flat plane covered by a hemisphere of stars set against a velvety black backdrop; ships could conceivably sail off the edge of the world, into a chasm where "there be dragons." To modern readers, however, the "world" is a sphere nearly 25,000 miles around in the midst of a single-star system on the fringe of the Milky Way Galaxy.

Context can make all the difference — and that's just the temporal element. We haven't even discussed cultural and personal biases yet. The various ancient scriptures were written in a variety of cultural and political settings. Some writers were members of the ruling class; others were repressed minorities. Some were subjects of tribal chieftains, others of kings, still others of emperors. Some lived in desert climates; others dwelt on fertile plains. One thing they all have in common: None was anything like the modern American or European cultures, through whose lenses they are most commonly interpreted.

Then, there's personal context. It's possible to plant "false facts" in someone's head or distort their memories by introducing new information that either augments or contradicts the initial data. If this new information comes from a trusted source, the recipient will likely second-guess his original conclusions and revise them to conform with that source's version of events. In this case, we no longer have an uncontaminated eyewitness account, but rather an account the blends personal recollection with what amounts to hearsay from a second source.

This is precisely why judges often sequester juries until they reach a verdict in criminal cases. They also order jurors not to investigate the issues raised in court on their own, and they prohibit panelists from following the case they're deciding in the media. They don't want the supposedly "pure" evidence presented in the courtroom contaminated with secondary suppositions and speculation.

It's only reasonable to ask whether the biblical accounts have been so contaminated.

Well, to start with, the earliest of the gospels was written about three decades after the events it purports to describe. Imagine if we were just now finding out that Ronald Reagan won the 1980 election and John Lennon was dead. That's roughly the same amount of time that passed between the tenure of Pontius Pilate as prefect of Judea and the initial publication of Mark's gospel. The author himself, if the gospel's attribution is to be believed, was a follower of Paul rather than Jesus. We can therefore expect him to have been influenced by Paul's theology and writings, some of which have been dated fifteen or twenty years earlier than the gospel. It's also quite possible that the gospel is anonymous, and that Mark's name was simply chosen to give it added credibility — the way Latter-day Saints founder Joseph Smith ascribed his revelation to some never-produced golden tablets he supposedly received from an angel. In this case, there's no way of knowing who influenced the author in the three decades that passed between Pilate's tenure and the gospel's production. Unless he was a hermit, he must have talked to some people during that time. And, presumably, since the topic of Jesus' life was of such interest to him, he spoke concerning that subject.

And got feedback.

And altered his perceptions based on that feedback — perhaps only slightly, perhaps without even knowing it, but altered them nonetheless.

Things become even more problematic for the authors of Matthew and Luke, both of whom incorporate (borrow? plagiarize?) substantial amounts of material from the Gospel of Mark. Two of the other gospels relied heavily on material contained in the first. So we've come to the realm of hearsay evidence transmitted over the course of more than thirty years — in the case of Matthew and Luke, more like forty or fifty. The Gospel of John, as we've seen, was written even later.

'Their Statements Did Not Agree'

When all is said and done, we can discount writers of the synoptic gospels (Matthew, Mark and Luke) as eyewitnesses with a fair degree of certainty. But what about the individuals they describe? How reliable are *they* as witnesses to the events depicted in the gospels — most importantly, to the event described by Paul as the foundation that underpins all of Christian doctrine: the resurrection?

The question is, sadly for the Christian apologist, moot, because according to the earliest account *there were no witnesses* to the resurrection. According to the Gospel of Mark, Jesus is placed in a tomb one day, and a few days later, his body is gone. No one sees him get up and walk out; no one sees anyone move the body. No one sees anything happen at all. Three women arrive to anoint Jesus' body with spices and find the tomb is empty; a white-robed young man sitting nearby claims to know what happened, but his identity is never revealed and there's no way to verify his story. He doesn't even claim to have witnessed anything, but merely states that Jesus "has risen" without any personal claim to have seen anything.

And we call this an eyewitness account?

The author of Luke tells basically the same story, but he replaces the young men in Mark's version with *two* men wearing dazzling clothes. The author may have added a second witness for the same reason the Pharisees demanded that Jesus produce one: under Jewish law, it establishes a degree of authenticity. Moreover, their dazzling clothes are certainly more impressive than the simple white robe adorning Mark's single witness. The story clearly is becoming more entertaining, if not more believable. The two men are still anonymous, and there's still no way to verify their story.

So we move on to the Gospel of Matthew, whose author is clearly concerned about the lack of verifiable eyewitness testimony. He is even more concerned about a story in wide circulation that accused Jesus' disciples of stealing his body. According to Matthew's version of events, there *were* witnesses to the events surrounding the supposed resurrection — a contingent of Roman guards — and this was their story. The author seeks to discredit it by declaring that the guards *did*, in fact, witness the resurrection, but were bribed by the chief priests and elders into fabricating the "stolen body" scenario.

Once again, none of this is independently verifiable, and its lack of consistency with the other accounts of the same incident throws the entire narrative into question. For one thing, the author tells us that an earthquake hit the area *after* the arrival of the three women mentioned in Mark. This temblor dislodged a large rock that had been set against the tomb's entrance. In the Marcan account, there is no earthquake. In Luke's version, it occurs *before* the women arrive. Matthew further confuses matters by stating that a single "angel" (not two men or a single boy in white) is present at the tomb to confirm Jesus' resurrection. The three women, who have arrived, conveniently enough, before the earthquake, provide him with three additional eyewitnesses.

The author of John, for his part, says nothing about an earthquake and states that Mary Magdalene alone arrived at the tomb to find it empty. In this version, she finds *two angels* seated where Jesus' body had been. This is yet a fourth separate attempt to place witnesses at the scene. One boy. Two men. One angel. Two angels. No two versions agree. One cannot help but bring to mind Mark's statement that many people testified against Jesus at his trial, but their statements did not agree. Frankly, it's hard to imagine their testimony being any more confusing and contradictory than the testimony we're asked to believe about the resurrection.

In John's version, unlike the others, Mary is confronted with Jesus himself — though she fails to recognize him, mistaking him for the gardener. If her powers of observation are this poor, how can the author expect us to take her seriously as a witness?

The situation is similar in some respects to a scene presented by the author of Luke, who relates an incident in which two of Jesus' followers meet him on the road and sit down to have a meal with him — all, apparently, without realizing who he is! Instead, however, they supposedly have an epiphany after the fact. Like the men (or angels, or boy) at the tomb, they are nameless individuals, so there's absolutely no way to verify their story.

If we were to boil down all the conflicting accounts into their common elements, we'd be left with Jesus being placed in a tomb; a stone being lain over the entrance and subsequently rolled aside; the tomb being found empty; the presence of one nameless individual of disputed origin at the tomb; the presence of Mary Magdalene. That's it. From this common denominator we're supposed to conclude that

Jesus did something unprecedented in the annals of human history. Yet the evidence simply doesn't support it. No American courtroom would admit hearsay evidence from biased witnesses submitted thirty or more years after the fact, and if the Christian god can't meet the human standards of American jurisprudence, how can we expect it to meet the much higher standard of eternal, infallible truth?

A modern Christian apologist once wrote a couple of books under the title *Evidence That Demands a Verdict*. Unfortunately for him, the evidence presented in the gospels concerning the central event in Christianity is so flimsy that a verdict isn't even warranted. The sort of unsubstantiated claims and flimsy evidence presented by the defenders of the resurrection demands nothing so much as the case being thrown out of court.

If the resurrection story can't even meet the standard of proof required in an American court of law, what does that say for its reliability?

That question brings us back to Paul's initial assertion: "If Christ is not risen, our preaching is for naught!"

Agreed.

So why are so many preachers still preaching?

"Never let your sense of morals get in the way of doing what's right."

— Isaac Asimov

Eleven: The Morals of the Story

When I began this project, I was under no illusions that I would be able to prove or disprove the existence of a creator. That was not my intent, in any case. What I did hope to do was identify why religion — and monotheistic religion in particular — seems to have such an uncanny knack for spreading hatred, mistrust and bigotry wherever it goes.

The conquest and slaughter of indigenous peoples, all in the name of salvation.

The torture and execution of heretics in the name of orthodoxy.

The burning of books to guard against "false teachings."

The confiscation of property and selling of indulgences as a means for the priesthood to enrich itself.

The common rejoinder to the mention of such inexcusable acts is a plea not to blame the Christian god. Rather, we are told that the fault lies with fallible humans who are prone to such heinous actions because they are mired in original sin. Yet if faith in Jesus doesn't at least mitigate against this condition, what is the purpose of such faith? Is it merely the equivalent of a "Get Out of Jail Free" card in monopoly? If the Christian faith doesn't present itself as a means of overcoming human frailty, what good is it?

That might sound crass, but it's a legitimate question. If you are going to advertise your belief system as the difference between life and death, heaven and hell, you ought to be able to provide some kind of proof that it actually makes a difference. Are religious people more ethical than atheists? As it turns out, the answer is no. Attitudes toward lying on resumes, cheating on exams and plagiarizing reports were virtually the same among religious and nonreligious individuals who participated in a 1993 study conducted by the Josephson Institute of Ethics in Marina Del Rey, Calif., titled *Ethics, Values, Attitudes and Behaviors in America: the Impact of Religious Belief, Gender and Age.*

What about more serious offenses? A 1999 article by Steve Chapman of the Chicago Tribune notes that, at the time, weekly church attendance stood at 44 percent in America, 17 points higher than in Britain and more than twice as high as France's rate. In Sweden, the rate was a mere 4 percent … 11 times lower. Yet the murder rate in these countries showed the opposite of what one might expect: The U.S. rate was six times higher Britain's, seven times higher than France's and five times higher than Sweden's. Clearly, many churchgoing Americans are more interested in posting the Ten Commandments on courthouse walls than in actually *keeping* No. 6 on that list.

One difference between non-theists and Christians is the impetus behind their morality. Non-theists must find their moral compass within. They do what they feel is correct based on their own ethical determinations (or, alternatively, because they don't want to be penalized for transgressing civil law). Christian dogma, on the other hand, teaches that humanity is irreparably damaged by original sin. As Paul wrote his followers in Rome, "I do not do what I wish to do, but rather, that which I hate … and it is no longer I myself who do it, but the sin that dwells within me. I desire that which is good, yet lack the means to carry it out."

Or, to put it plainly, he's screwed without God.

The impetus behind Christian morality is therefore necessarily external. God gets the credit for both telling us what to do and giving us the strength to do it. Human beings are, in essence, merely along for the ride. If, however, this were the case, shouldn't we see some more tangible results among Christians? Shouldn't they behave better, because they have, as it were, God on their side?

One would think so.

Yet the emphasis on belief seems to make no difference. What does make a difference is one's moral code. This is where the folly of the belief-salvation mechanism is exposed for the fraud it really is. Jesus wasn't particularly concerned about Pauline ideals such as salvation by faith through grace. He developed an ethical system, passed it along to his followers and hoped (as most teachers do) that they had paid attention and would care enough to implement it in their own lives. If John's account is to be credited, Jesus taught a system of love expressed through action: "Whoever has my commands and keeps them, he is the one who loves me."

Many would find this a compelling statement. The moral system he developed left plenty of room to adapt to changing situations, so long as the overriding concern was love. How should that love be expressed? Jesus offered some guidelines in his famed Sermon on the Mount and other teachings, but he left his followers the flexibility to practice love according to the circumstances — those dreaded situational ethics. The Sabbath was made for man, not man for the Sabbath.

If one gives any credence to the teachings attributed to Jesus, it would stand to reason that following those teachings could be beneficial. Unfortunately, the Pauline dogma that was heaped on top of Jesus' teachings had the effect of relegating them to the status of background noise. The issue became not action, but simple belief. And simple belief, by itself, is not going to change anyone's moral behavior. As the author of James put it, even *demons* believe. That alone certainly doesn't make these rather unsavory characters any more ethical (fictional though they may be). The author of the epistle of James, a work attributed to Jesus' brother, also stated plainly that "faith without action is dead." Such sentiments almost got the book excluded from the canon, for they stood as a blatant contradiction to Paul's teachings about faith alone being both necessary and sufficient. And while the book was ultimately included, its message was still drowned out by Paul's rhetoric about the primacy of belief.

The old saying about finding a job applies to orthodox Christianity, as well: It's not what you know, it's who you know (actually, whom, but the saying isn't generally transmitted that way). It's much more about worshipping Jesus than it is about following his teachings. In fact, if you suggest that Jesus was a "great moral teacher," orthodox Christians will take offense and say you're blaspheming. What most people would view as a compliment, they consider an insult — and one worthy of eternal damnation, at that. They don't find salvation in Jesus' teachings, but rather in the primitive and absurd idea that he offered himself up as a ritual sacrifice for the sins of humankind. If these sins were really *that* bad, however, he wouldn't have been doing anyone a favor. Imagine some philosophy professor offering to take Charles Manson's place in prison. Quite a few people would object on the grounds that they wouldn't want a maniacal mass murderer running loose in polite society.

If people keep on sinning despite this grand gesture, as the research quoted earlier indicates they do, Jesus' sacrifice constitutes pretty much the same thing — the Get Out of Jail Free card referred to earlier. You get to avoid the punishment you deserve, but you're not required to change your behavior a whit. Personal responsibility goes out the window, and you get a VIP seat on Cloud No. 9 after you die.

The doctrine of hell, by the way, *has* been attributed to Jesus, which could indicate that not all of his teachings were particularly enlightened. But in the black-and-white world of orthodox Christendom, it's either one extreme or the other: sinful wretches are let loose to wreak havoc on the world based simply on a confession of faith, or they're consigned to a fiery furnace for all eternity if they fail to make such a confession. What ever happened to the punishment fitting the crime?

Cult of Personality

What orthodox Christian dogma has done, effectively, is hijack a belief system based on certain moral standards, gut it and replace it with a single commandment: not Jesus' injunction to follow his example, but Paul's mandate to accept the gift of grace. The formula is simple: "Believe in the Lord Jesus, and you shall be saved — you and all your household" (Acts 16:31). In setting forth this doctrine, Paul placed moral responsibility for members of an entire household on the shoulders of a single individual — yet another biblical assault on personal responsibility. But what's even worse is the resulting transformation of a moral code into a cult of personality.

The human tendency to put leaders on a pedestal is well documented. Not only do we worship gods we deem infallible, we place the same burden on our heroes. Jesus is perhaps the best example. It's not enough — or even necessary — that we follow his teachings. We must, rather, worship him as God incarnate, the sinless and infallible manifestation of the creator of the universe. If we live our lives in accord with everything he taught, yet fail to do this thing, we are screwed. If, on the other hand, we flout every single one of his teachings, yet acknowledge him as "lord and savior," we're in like Flynn (or is it Flint?).

The Qur'an, to its credit, explicitly states that Muhammad is *not* to be worshipped: "Muhammad is only a messenger, and many messengers have passed away before him" (3:144). Elsewhere, the text identifies some of these messengers, referring to "what has been revealed to Abraham and Ishmael and Isaac and Jacob and their descendants, and what was given to Moses and Jesus, and to the prophets of the Lord. We make no distinction between any of them"

(2:136). None of this, however, has stopped Muslims from venerating Muhammad and exalting him far above the status of the other messengers mentioned in this text. As the prophet to the Arab peoples, he was one of them. Because he epitomized the pious Arab servant of Allah, he in a sense came to represented them all. Apart from Ishmael, a shadowy figure of legend of whom little is known, Muhammad is the one figure in the prophetic tradition Arabs can claim to be one of their own.

This is enormously important, it seems, to the human psyche. It appears natural for us to choose a human symbol to represent ourselves as a whole, either as an ethnic group or a species. In the United States, many in the African American community view Martin Luther King Jr. in this light; some in the Latino/Hispanic community, particularly on the West Coast, similarly exalt the memory of farm labor activist Cesar Chavez. Buddhists can point to the Dalai Lama; Catholics to Mother Teresa and a whole host of saints; the gay and lesbian community to Harvey Milk.

Each of these individuals was a living, breathing person. In the case of the Dalai Lama, he still is. Yet time and distance cloud our memories, and we tend to distill the essence of who they were down into a few choice impressions, which we then tend to magnify. We exchange fallible, three-dimensional people for cardboard cutouts that dispense with all the messy details. Like the fact that Mother Teresa once confided, "There is such terrible darkness within me, as if everything was dead. It has been there more or less from the time I started 'the work.' " Anything but a ringing endorsement of the church's mission. Then there are the accusations of plagiarism and adultery that followed Dr. King.

As for the Dalai Lama, he has reportedly condemned homosexuality but endorsed prostitution — as long as the customer pays up.

Chavez, for his part, was reportedly influenced by Synanon, a cult-like group that exposed its members to a form of abuse that amounted to severe hazing and public humiliation. According to

Randy Shaw, author of the Chavez biography *Beyond the Fields*, the legendary labor organizer sought to adapt this "Game," as it was called, to ensure loyalty within his United Farm Workers union. Synanon itself was only a step away from Jim Jones' People's Temple. Some who dared to leave the group were beaten, and a reporter who fought to expose it was bitten by a rattlesnake that had been placed in his mailbox. He nearly died. Synanon itself eventually disbanded when it ran afoul of the IRS and had to sell off all its assets.

None of this is meant to diminish the positive and, in some cases, monumental accomplishments of these individuals. It is meant simply to illustrate the fact that these individuals were not perfect, any more than Muhammad, Jesus or any other human being has been perfect. Yet their human admirers all too easily — and eagerly — apply the black-and-white tendency of theism to the mortal realm as well. It's simply easier to think of things, and people, in absolute terms. Or maybe we just never outgrow our childhood fantasies that Prince Charming will ride up on a white horse to rescue us, or that the perfect princess will fall head over heels for our froggy selves, opening a divine portal to Happily Ever After. We often seem unable, or unwilling, to consider the truth of the matter: that those who are exceptional are, nonetheless, imperfect, and that those who are deeply flawed — or even downright malicious — still aren't evil incarnate. To ignore the complexities of human behavior and ethics is to diminish the richness of humanity itself. We place our heroes on pedestals incapable of bearing the weight of their finitude, and we consign our villains to the eternal flames of an imaginary dungeon of our own design.

This is the nature of the hell we've created, all because our heroes must all be Superman and our villains all Voldemort.

When we deify our heroes, we do them a grave disservice. We focus on their supposed divinity at the expense of their messages and the examples that they set. Indeed, we may even start to think we don't need to follow those teachings or examples because they've already done all the work for us. Moreover, we can't possibly follow their example, even should we wish to, because these people were more than human. They had an ability we lack to pull the very god of the universe down from the sky, bind him within their mortal frames and perform feats that no ordinary mortal could possibly emulate.

That, however, undermines the very ideals most such individuals champion. These exceptional individuals, without exception, recognized they could not achieve their vision alone.

They were not gods.

Martin Luther King Jr.'s first line of his famous "I Have a Dream" speech: "I am happy *to join with you* today in what will go down in history as the greatest demonstration for freedom in the history of our nation."

Cesar Chavez: "The answer *lies with you and me*. It is with *all men and women* who share the suffering and yearn with us for a better world."

Harvey Milk: "The young gay people in the Altoona, Pennsylvanias and the Richmond, Minnesotas. .... The only thing they have to look forward to is hope. *And you have to give them hope.* Hope for a better world, hope for a better tomorrow, hope for a better place to come to if the pressures at home are too great."

The italics in each case are mine. These are not the words of infallible beings, but of humans seeking to motivate other humans to action. They are not the words of men looking for others to revere or believe in or worship them, but of men seeking to share a message they believed to be profoundly important to their listeners and the world at large. The message, the good news, was bigger than the person delivering it. For each of the speakers quoted above, that message was justice and equality. The same might be said for Jesus, who counseled his followers to judge not, lest they be judged in equal measure.

"My problem lies in reconciling my gross habits with my net income."

— Errol Flynn

Twelve: The Charlatan's Web

Is monotheism immoral?

Amoral?

Or just confusing as hell?

Sometimes it's hard to tell. But what seems clear from our investigation so far is that it's no more ethical than atheism and may, in some senses, even be less so. The problem lies in the fact that monotheism doesn't promote morality but, rather, relegates it to a place of secondary importance behind worship. If the worship of the one god conflicts with moral precepts — even the precepts set down in the name of this god himself — there's no question what takes precedence. One must follow the dictates of the god (or, more precisely, the priests and prophets who presume to speak on his behalf) regardless of whether they accord with the moral teachings of the deity, his son or his scriptures. The examples that illustrate this tendency are too many to mention. But here are a few, some of which we've already covered:

- Yahweh condemns murder, then commands Abraham to kill his only son.
- Yahweh proclaims he does not delight in sacrifices, then arranges to have *his* only son killed … as a sacrifice.
- Yahweh states that the soul who has sinned is the one who shall die … after condemning David's *son* to death for the king's adulterous tryst with Bath-Sheba.
- Allah commands his followers to fight those who do not believe in him, yet also tells them to forgive these same individuals.
- Yahweh commands that his followers honor their parents on pain of death, but Jesus demands that his followers be willing to forsake their parents to follow him.

Who benefits from these contradictory statements? The clergy and the prophets, who have appointed themselves as arbiters of faith, supremely qualified to sort it all out. It's not that they're actually any better at it than we are. A contradiction is a contradiction, and no individual — divinely appointed or otherwise — has access to any sort of secret logic that will allow a human being to reconcile two mutually exclusive statements. Talk about mysteries and paradoxes all you want; it simply can't be done.

In a system that acknowledges situational nuances in an ever-changing reality, one could argue that homicide is appropriate under some circumstances. In self-defense, for instance. Or, perhaps, as a means of saving other lives. Yet, in what can be described as an ironic reversal of fortune, it's doubtful that most of the so-called "moral relativists" so roundly condemned by the theists would condone an act of human sacrifice to propitiate a vengeful deity. It simply doesn't fit within their moral compass.

And contradictory commands to simultaneously turn left and right, partake and abstain, condemn and forgive, don't fit within his (or her) rational framework, either.

But it does fit perfectly with into the strategy of the priestly class.

If everything were simple and straightforward, what need would there be for a priesthood? If the laity were able to figure everything out for themselves, they'd give the priests and prophets a pink slip and send them packing without severance pay. The powers that be couldn't have that. So they developed a system so absurd and convoluted no one on earth could possibly make sense of it without the "proper guidance."

Their guidance.

Step one: Present an insoluble puzzle to an unsuspecting target audience — people looking for some semblance of meaning in their lives. Step two: When they become frustrated in their attempts to solve that puzzle, swoop down and offer to assume the burden for them. Such a magnanimous gesture will be gratefully accepted and … mission accomplished. They've got you right where they want you, in the palm of your grubby little hand. Think this is farfetched? Just fill in the blanks. First, provide the insoluble problem. That would be Paul's doctrine of original sin. Then supply the secret, magic solution: the death of Jesus on a cross. And voila! Accept the solution, and you get eternal life; reject it, and you get shunted off where to a pit of fire.

Doesn't this seem just a tiny bit sadistic?

A Piece of the Action

When you boil it down into its simplest terms, it seems like nothing so much as a glorified schoolyard strong-arm job, in which the bully "politely" asks his victim to turn over his school lunch money or his Air Jordans.

An even better analogy is the tried-and-true mob protection racket, operated here on a massive scale. For those unfamiliar with the concept, a crime boss or some of his henchmen pay a "friendly visit" to retail businesses in the neighborhood and offer to provide "protection" against whatever vandals, armed robbers and other unseemly characters happen to be in the area. What's left unsaid is that the aforementioned vandals, robbers and thugs are under the employ of the syndicate itself. The crime boss is extorting a fee from the businesses as insurance that his own men won't trash the premises, clean out the till and harass the customers. If you don't pay up, they'll shut you down.

In the same way these ruffians extract payment from the helpless businessmen in their "territory," the clergy operate a shakedown of the congregants in their parish. You pay the syndicate to protect you from … the syndicate. And you pay the church to protect you from its own dogma. Hell. Original sin. The devil. It's all the same racket. There's as much evidence for hell and original sin as there is for the invisible hoodlums from whom you supposedly need protection — according to the syndicate. These independent criminals simply don't exist (the syndicate wouldn't allow them to operate in its territory even if they did).

Now, do you really think an all-powerful god would let some two-bit hustler like the devil operate in his territory?

Not a chance.

But what his priests will do is let you *think* he's a threat as an excuse to offer you their protection in the form of sanctification, forgiveness of sins and even, in extreme cases, exorcisms. For a fee. First, you have to let them keep an eye on you via confessions and regular attendance at their gatherings. More importantly, however, you have to give them a piece of the action. The standard cut is ten percent, as prescribed under the Mosaic law. It always seemed peculiar to me that this particular mandate, which wasn't even important enough to make the Old Testament top ten, has been so carefully preserved and applied — religiously — under a "new" covenant that supposedly replaced an old one described as "obsolete and outdated" (Heb. 8:13).

The syndicate isn't really in any position to "protect" the mom-and-pop stores on its turf from anybody, nor does it have any interest in doing so. Its only real interest is enriching itself at the expense of neighborhood business owners, lining its pockets without really doing any work. Similarly, the priests and profits … er … prophets

… of the church's protection racket don't have any special ability to protect their flocks from the devil.

There's an old saying, popularized by the movie *The Usual Suspects* and repeated frequently in some Christian circles, that "the greatest trick the devil ever pulled was convincing the world he didn't exist."

I disagree.

The greatest trick the church ever pulled was convincing the world he *did*.

Once you have a bogeyman to strike fear into your target audience, all you have to do is present yourself (or your god) as a savior destined to defeat him. But not too quickly, because you need him. If the devil were actually defeated, the church would lose a powerful weapon it has used to control millions upon millions of people over the centuries. Satan serves a powerful purpose: He provides a focal point, a common enemy — a scapegoat. Regimes worried about internal divisions often invoke Satan as a means of distracting their citizens from such inconvenient truths as human rights abuses, poverty, repression and so forth. They take all those pent-up frustrations and redirect them toward some external "threat." European kings saw the Crusades as just such an opportunity. In modern times, an overtly Christian president of the United States identified three nations as an "axis of evil" while the nation's economy was barreling toward a massive recession. Meanwhile, the ayatollahs of Iran have branded the United States as "the Great Satan," even as they repress their own citizens with strict forms of Sharia law.

If you can't — or don't wish to — deal with anger over domestic injustice, simply blame the scapegoat and relieve the pressure.

The author of the first epistle of John stated unequivocally that "perfect love casts out fear" (1 John 4:18). Yet the church has a vested interest in maintaining an attitude of fear for precisely the reason stated above. Indeed, it has seemed more at home with fear than love throughout much of its history. Inquisitions, torture chambers, persecutions and forced conversions have often been the rule rather than the exception. If perfect love casts out fear, one has to ask whether the converse is true: Does extreme fear banish love? And if so, what takes its place? Cowering obedience? A poor substitute, most would say, for freely given love. Yet if such love is not forthcoming, it is the wont of abusive and controlling individuals to extract, by threat and force if necessary, the thing that seems on its surface to be the nearest approximation.

This very process is itself driven by fear.

Fear of losing control.

Fear of being invalidated.

Fear of feeling naked and alone in a universe very much different than what you thought it was.

This is the very fear that drives the church to its most inhuman acts and most heinous crimes. Deep down, the clergy who claim to have a better handle on the universe and a closer relationship with the divine know, or at least suspect, that it may all be hogwash. And that terrifies them. Mother Teresa once told a spiritual confidant: "Jesus has a very special love for you. As for me, the silence and the emptiness is so great, that I look and do not see — listen and do not hear — the tongue moves, but does not speak. I want you to pray for me." And Jesus himself, at a moment celebrated by Christianity, cried out, "My god! My god! Why have you forsaken me?" as he hung on the cross.

What if, in the end, it's all for naught? What if there is no god, no salvation, no hope of eternal life? What if the entire thing turns out to be a lie? The weight of such a possibility can be almost too much to bear. It must be beaten back, by any means necessary. The best way for believers to reinforce their own precarious faith, to gird themselves against their own insidious doubts, is to assuage them by finding — or creating — other true believers.

"Compel them to come in." This was the solution proposed by Augustine of Hippo, a man who himself was alternately wracked by doubts and resolute in suppressing them — both in himself and others. Augustine spent his youth as a typical seeker and randy young man. By day, he tried out one philosophical system after another, as if each were a new outfit he hoped would fit better than the last. By night, he enjoyed the comforts of the flesh. At seventeen, he took a concubine who bore him a son, but though she remained with him for the next thirteen years, he couldn't bring himself to marry her because she was beneath his social class. Meanwhile, he studied the writings of Cicero and became an adherent of Manichaeism, a dualistic system influenced by Gnostic thinking that the mainstream church rejected as heretical.

On a trip to Milan, however, he became exposed to the teachings of the orthodox bishop Ambrose and grew more open to the school of thought he was promoting. He spurned his concubine — the mother of his child — only to take up again with a different woman. In despair over his doubts and sense of guilt, he reported crying out to the heavens and hearing in answer what seemed like a child's voice chanting, "Take and read! Take and read!" Dutifully, he opened a collection of Paul's epistles and found himself confronted with the following passage:

"Not in carousing and drunkenness, not in sexual lusts and immorality, not in strife and envy, but rather clothe yourselves in the Lord Christ Jesus, and make no provision for the lusts of the flesh" (Rom. 13:13-14).

To hear Augustine tell it, someone might have switched on a light bulb — had such a device been invented at the time — and he had no need to read any further. In that moment, he proclaimed, "all the shadows of doubt were dispelled."

Augustine's choice of Paul's masterwork as his inspiration was both telling and portentous. Telling because he, like Paul, experienced a conversion that was both abrupt and decisive. Portentous because he would use Paul's teachings as a template to develop in full the heinous doctrines that those teachings demanded when taken to their logical end. But such sudden and complete conversions are seldom what they seem. The doubts expressed prior to such epiphanies are seldom simply swept away as shadows, to use Augustine's metaphor, but remain beneath the surface, forcibly repressed lest they challenge the latest object of faith to which the seeker has attached himself. Anyone who reads Paul's writings cannot help but be keenly aware of the man's elaborate rationalizations and extreme defensiveness — clear marks of someone whose doubts persist, despite his fondest hope of certitude.

The same was true of Augustine, who despite his protestations to the contrary, continued to struggle so mightily with his own doubt that he tried to account or it by proclaiming that "doubt is but another element of faith."

The full measure of Augustine's philosophical contortions is well beyond the scope of this work. Suffice to say, however, that he did, in fact, distort and pervert Jesus' simple parable of the wedding banquet from the Gospel of Matthew as a justification for forced conversion. Speaking of the Donatists, members of a sect identified as heretical by Augustine and his orthodox compatriots, he counseled: "Compel them to come in." By force of threat, by force of arms, by any means necessary. One cannot help but suspect that the rage Augustine unleashed against the Donatists made them scapegoats for his own pent-up resentment toward the doubts that lingered inside him. Doubts he refused to acknowledge. The only way to continue repressing them was to rid himself of any external reminder of their existence — of any way of thinking that challenged his own.

In so doing, he ushered in an era of conquests and forced conversions during which countless others after him twisted Jesus' words to the same vile purpose. Unable to squelch their own doubts, they exterminated those who dared express them. In doing so, they not only eliminated the competition, they also bolstered the church's numbers and buoyed its confidence in the delusions it had wrought. As the saying goes, "Two billion people can't be wrong."

There's strength and safety in numbers, and the bandwagon affect is a powerful motivator, especially when those riding the bandwagon are carrying sawed-off shotguns and pitchforks. It was not the eloquence of reason that persuaded so many people to join the church. It was a combination of threats, peer pressure and nastiness that took the form of pogroms, witch hunts and executions. Once the phenomenon had grown to encompass the vast majority of people in a given culture, it was a matter simple inevitability. You were a Christian because of where and to whom you were born; there was simply no other alternative. It was as final and constricting as the caste system on the Indian subcontinent.

Ignoring Jesus' teaching that his kingdom was not of this world, Augustine and his followers set out to establish an earthly "City of God" and, for a time at least, succeeded. Plenty of believers wish to accomplish the same, even today.

It is God's will, they say, and who are you, o man, to question the almighty?

Might, indeed, makes right.

Just ask your local crime syndicate.

And money sustains that might.

Maximizing Prophets

Praise the Lord and pass the offering plate. There's a reason they call it the *almighty* dollar. It can buy friends, power, fame and a damned nice sanctuary for your megachurch congregation. Or a gallery of beautiful stained glass windows for your cathedral. Say what you will about the Catholic church and its wayward stepchildren, the evangelical Protestants. They know how to dress up a church building: padded pews, weighty architecture, grand pianos, marble floors, wood inlays, plush carpeting, snazzy baptismal fit for Sea World. The works.

Nothing's too good for the house of God.

The European cathedrals of the middle ages were meant to evoke a sense of awe and wonder, with the sunlight gleaming through the multicolored glass and the soaring archways that draw the gaze upward toward heaven.

All the trappings.

But what of the substance? That's where things get tricky. It's not that the emperor has no clothes; rather, the clothes adorn a phantom emperor. It is, to resort to an overused cliché, all style and no substance. With all this grandeur and over-the-top ornamentation, there must be something to it. Even Oz, in all its glory, had a man behind the curtain. But the holy of holies in the Jewish temple was notoriously empty, and the same might be said for the claims and threats made by the modern church.

It takes money to sustain such illusions, especially when the reality is considerably starker and less inspiring. And the illusions are not merely physical, but spiritual as well. They might consist of golden tablets that no one else can see. They might involve the illusion of a televangelist "healing" a perfectly healthy actor planted in the audience by the show's producer. They might be found in a piece of wood from the "true cross" that can change your life for the better, or in a promise that a small (or not so small) indulgence can shorten your time in purgatory.

Defenders of the faith might argue that these are abuses of power, that they're the exceptions rather than the rule. Yet such chicanery has, indeed, occurred. Its practitioners have admitted to it, its critics have exposed it, and film crews have even documented it. Can the same be said of the claims made concerning presumably "legitimate" miracles? In point of fact, there's far more proof that the fakers are faking it than there is of any genuine articles performing authentic signs and wonders.

That's problematic for the clergy, who need to perpetuate the notion that they have superior access to heaven. Their failure to do so is nothing short of catastrophic. It not only exposes them as charlatans but renders them immediately irrelevant to the god-man dynamic. Without such proof, one could eliminate the middleman and proceed directly to the throne of heaven — presuming, of course, that such a place exists and isn't yet another illusion perpetuated to keep the powerful in power.

Strip away the cathedrals, the stained glass, the dubious miracles and the golden candelabra. What's left?

Nothing but a bunch of self-important men in flowing robes, fancy suits, skullcaps and bad toupees staring back at you from in front of an altar or behind your TV screen. Human beings. Nothing more. People with no greater access to the god they claim to worship than the "common folk" they're bamboozling with their fancy accoutrements, grand cathedrals and false claims. If they were any closer to heaven than the masses, they'd be able to demonstrate their exalted position to the divine in some sort of empirical sense, by performing more miracles, coming up with more accurate (and specific) prophecies, providing greater insights or, at the very least, more sound advice than the lowly laity. I'm not aware of a single study that confirms they can do any of this, yet they continue to make the claim, and offer up illusions in lieu of solid evidence.

"The zeal which begins with hypocrisy must conclude in treachery; at first it deceives, at last it betrays."

— Francis Bacon Sr.

Thirteen: Whoa, Pharisee!

It's particularly astonishing that such vain and self-important individuals continue to perpetrate their hoaxes on the public in light of Jesus' famous rant excoriating the Pharisees for the very same sort of behavior in his own day. The parallels are brought up from time to time among church folk, but are mostly mentioned in a perfunctory manner, with an implied wink and a nod, because nothing ever changes once the Bible study passes on — to the relief of the clergy, no doubt — to the next section of the gospel.

Though they're no doubt familiar to many readers, it's worthwhile to revisit them here, if solely for the purpose of not allowing the modern hypocrites to get away with the sort of behavior Jesus refused to accept in his own day. He warned the crowds of men who "do not practice what they preach — they tie up heavy, unwieldy burdens and place them on people's shoulders, yet they themselves are unwilling to lift a finger to move them."

Heavy, unwieldy burdens. That sounds a lot like Paul's doctrine of original sin, for starters. One can't get much heavier or more unwieldy than the idea that you are hopelessly infected with a so-called sinful nature for which there is no cure. You can ask for and receive forgiveness from an invisible god (or his self-appointed and quite visible representatives on earth), but they can't or won't do anything about the problem. Talk about treating the symptom and avoiding the root of the problem.

If there even is such a problem.

One has to marvel at the implications of this. The person of Jesus, who is depicted as nothing so clearly as a healer, is evidently powerless or unwilling to heal humans of this condition. It's hard to tell which conclusion is more disturbing: Either a god-man with unlimited power has declined to remedy the situation, or the most famous healer of all time found it beyond his power to do so. Imagine the foremost physician in the world comes to visit you in your hospital bed, announces you're terminally ill, then declares he won't be taking your case. He holds in his hand a potential cure, but instead of administering it takes out a salt shaker and proceeds to lavishes the contents on your open sores. But he "forgives" you for getting sick. He then expects you to thank him for taking the time out of his busy schedule to see you. He's important, after all.

The Pharisees, like our self-important doctor, were attention hogs. "Everything they do is done for people to see. They make their prayer boxes expansive and the tassels on their garments long. They love to take the most prominent places banquets and the seats of greatest honor in the synagogues." People who want to draw attention to themselves tend to be insecure. They need affirmation to confirm their sense of self-worth, and they need to remain highly visible to feel important and powerful. What's more visible than a place at an ornate altar in a magnificent cathedral? Or a picture-perfect set piece in a Hollywood studio, whence you're beamed into millions of homes every Sunday?

Jesus continued: "Woe to you teachers of the law and Pharisees! Hypocrites! You shut the door of heaven's kingdom in people's faces. You yourselves do not enter, nor will you allow those to enter who seek to do so."

This is the perfect insight into the mindset so often employed by religious elites. They "do not enter" because they refuse to follow the moral principles that their founder set down. Then they keep others from entering by replacing those principles with rules designed to keep them in positions of power — frequently rules that line their own pockets and help them maintain their advantage: tithing, indulgences, and the rest of the usual suspects.

"Woe to you! Blind guides! You say that if anyone swears by the temple, it means nothing, but the one who swears by the gold in the temple is bound by that oath. You blind fools! Which is greater: the gold or the temple that sanctifies it?"

Here, Jesus indicts the Pharisees for their love of what the King James version refers to as mammon. To quote the title of a well-known hip-hop single by Puff Daddy, "It's all about the Benjamins."

At least the Pharisees were honest.

They apparently admitted that money was more important to them than the temple or the altar on which the offerings were placed. That's more than can be said for most modern priests of mammon, who stridently argue that their money goes to do "the work of the Lord," even as many of them drive around in luxury cars and pile up personal fortunes that would have made most Pharisees drool. To be fair, some churches use much of the money they collect for worthy causes, but there are those that still plow their profits into buttressing the ostentatious façade they've created to impress the faithful. Millions are spent on religious theme parks, museums dedicated to the myth of "intelligent design" and gobs of makeup and mascara to withstand the white-hot lights of the TV studio.

The modern day televangelist, like his predecessor the Pharisee, has a definite problem with priorities.

"Woe to you, teachers of the law and Pharisees! Hypocrites! You give a tenth of your spices — your mint and dill and cumin. Yet you neglect the more important aspects of the law — justice and mercy and faithfulness. You should have practiced the latter without neglecting the former. Blind guides! You strain out a gnat, yet swallow a camel!"

Do you have that picture in your head? Now try not to laugh.

Beyond the comical analogy of some poor sap chowing down on a dromedary, however, Jesus is taking the Pharisees to task over the serious issue of priorities. Many a preacher has seized on Jesus' injunction not to neglect "the former" as an excuse to ignore the broader intent of his reprimand. But to do so entirely misses the point. The issues Jesus identifies as "more important" are all matters of broad principle, not specific directives. Each one can — and indeed must — be interpreted in the context of a given situation. That's a camel compared to the gnat of specific, nitpicky regulations. Since so many modern Christians like to take the Bible literally, let's make a literal comparison here: An adult male dromedary can weigh as much as two thousand pounds. A gnat, by contrast, weighs far less than an ounce. So, being generous, it would take 32,000 gnats piled one on top of the other to equal the weight of the camel.

Of course, Jesus was speaking metaphorically, not literally. But the point was exactly the same: to illustrate the yawning chasm that separated the first "gnatty" class of commands — specifically including, we should note, the tithe — from the second.

Are the same upside-down priorities in place today? All one has to do is look at the monuments to luxury and decadence that are so many churches to see that the answer is "yes." If tithing were given its appropriate gnat-sized place in a church service, the basket wouldn't be passed around, but would merely be made available upon request. There's an easy way to tell a church's motivations for soliciting money: simply listen to *why* the pastor says you should give. If he's honest, he'll tell you the money is needed for a specific purpose, whether it be to feed the hungry in Kenya, keep the lights on or pay his salary. If he's trying to manipulate you, he'll pull out the tithe commandment, basically telling you to give "because God says so." Not only does that approach expose such a solicitor as a modern-day Pharisee, but it also runs directly counter to Paul's views on the subject: "Each of you should give what you have determined to give, not reluctantly or under compulsion" (2 Cor. 9:7). Or under duress. More on that subject a bit later. The fact is, invoking the Old Testament law amounts to compulsion. And simply because the money is going to a religious institution, it doesn't mean that institution has the right to avoid being honest and transparent about its financial practices. As with any other charity, donors have a right to see a full accounting of how the money is spent.

Jesus' next two complaints against the Pharisees were similar: "You clean the outside of the cup and of the dish, while the inside is filled with greed and self-indulgence." And this: "You are like whitewashed tombs, which look beautiful on the outside while the interior is brimming hypocrisy and wickedness."

A plainer indictment style over substance could scarcely be imagined. The style, of course, is paid for with those tithes … and with the riches that supposedly make it harder or a person to enter the kingdom of heaven than it is to force a camel through the eye of a needle.

Jesus goes on to condemn the Pharisees for rejecting the prophets, sages and teachers: "Some of them you kill and crucify; others you flog in your assembly houses and stalk from town to town. … You kill the prophets and stone those sent to you." Jesus' words didn't seem to have the least effect on future generations who claimed to be his followers. You may ask, "Which prophets did they reject?"

Galileo Galilei was forced to recant his conclusion that Earth orbited the sun when he was found "vehemently suspect of heresy" because his conclusions were in conflict with church teachings. Goirdano Bruno, an astronomer, philosopher and Dominican friar who lived in the latter half of the 16th century, postulated that the sun was actually a star. He was ultimately burned at the stake for this and other beliefs the church found distasteful, among them a belief in pantheism — the idea that God is present in all of nature rather than a separate entity with remarkably human characteristics sitting on a throne amidst the clouds. This same philosophy got Baruch Spinoza of Amsterdam in hot water during the 17th century, though not with the Catholic Church but with another strand of monotheism: the Jewish community of which he was a member. This community cursed him in no uncertain terms and forbade anyone to "communicate with him, verbally or in writing, nor show him any favour, nor stay under the same roof with him, nor be within four cubits of him, nor read anything composed or written by him."

All this when he was just 23 years old.

Several scientists in the late 19th century were condemned by various churchmen for daring to investigate the geology behind the supposed worldwide flood of Noah. When they arrived at conclusions that did not gibe with church dogma, they were accused of engaging in "a dark art" that was "not a subject of lawful inquiry." Then there's the famous (or infamous, depending on one's viewpoint) Charles Darwin, whose theory of evolution has largely avoided any slings and arrows from the Catholic quarter but has been assailed with great tenacity by Protestants, particularly American evangelicals.

William Jennings Bryan, who ran unsuccessfully for president three times and took the creationist side (equally unsuccessfully) in the famous Scopes Trial just before his death, declared with an unabashed flourish of hyperbole that "all the ills from which America suffers can be traced to the teaching of evolution." Nearly a century later, American politicians and preachers are still blasting away at Darwin's ideas with equal vehemence.

Jesus was entirely correct to point out the hypocrisy of the Pharisees, who reportedly said, "If we had lived in the days of our forebears, we would not have joined with them in shedding the blood of the prophets." Hindsight, as they say, is 20-20, but prophets tend to announce impending change or unpleasant news. Both are threats of direst sort in the eyes of the religious establishment. Anything that challenges the carefully crafted and lovingly preserved status quo is to be opposed with both barrels.

It can hardly be coincidence that religious traditions tend to identify their respective founders as the *last* in the line of prophets. The ultimate. In Christianity, Jesus identified himself as a prophet indirectly when he said, "No prophet is accepted in his hometown." Or, he might have added, in his own day. But Christians have hesitated to identify Jesus as a prophet, for fear that it would diminish his status below the rank of divine god-man. In consequence, they have chosen to identify his immediate predecessor, John the Baptizer, as the last in the line of prophets. This man, not coincidentally, is depicted in the gospels as explicitly endorsing Jesus. Islam, similarly, ends the line of prophets with its founder, Muhammad. Mani, the founder of Manichaeism, also identified himself as the last prophet or "seal of the prophets." Among the Jews, the prophetic tradition ended with Malachi.

This practice of cutting of the prophetic line amounts to the theological equivalent of having the last word. It allows the founder of a new religion to accomplish two things: First, he enhances his credibility by associating himself with a prophetic heritage that dates back centuries. He's not just some random yokel spouting off ideas from left field; he's firmly anchored in a long tradition that's already recognized by the culture in which he's operating.

On the other hand, he is also the last in this illustrious tradition, making him the ultimate arbiter of truth. It doesn't always turn out this way: Moses, not Malachi, is considered the greatest prophet of Judaism, for example. But that's the exception rather than the rule.

What it all comes down to is a desire to set things down in stone, as Moses supposedly did — to force the wheel of continual change to a grinding halt by the sheer force of will and a deep bass baritone voice from heaven. It's a desire expressed in scriptural texts, as well: Consider the final words inscribed by the author of the Book of Revelation:

"I issue this warning to all those who hear the words of the prophecy contained in this scroll: If anyone adds anything to them, God will add to such a one the plagues described herein. And if anyone removes words from this scroll of prophecy, God will remove from such a one any share in the tree of life and the holy city described herein" (Rev. 22:18-19).

Believers often apply this curse to the whole of the Bible, though its author clearly meant it to cover his own work specifically. If the entire canon of scripture were meant, such threats obviously had little effect. The likes of Marcion, Muhammad and Joseph Smith either added to or subtracted from the library of "revealed scripture" with impunity over the centuries.

Unfortunately for those who seek to stop the march of progress for their own convenience and self-aggrandizement, things just don't work that way. As long as the world continues to evolve, Darwinian style, new prophets will always arise. They'll be rejected, perhaps killed and ultimately revered as visionaries by later generations who recognize their contributions — and who say, along with the Pharisees of Jesus' day, that they would never have done what their forbears did.

Even as they pick up stones to emulate them.

"Those who can make you believe absurdities, can make you commit atrocities."

– Voltaire

Fourteen: Atheists in Foxholes

Theists like to say there are no atheists in foxholes. Every time I hear this phrase, a little voice in the back of my head mutters, "Is this the best you can do?"

Of all the arguments I've heard for theism, this is perhaps the most simplistic and the least credible. I'm not on my deathbed yet, so I have no way of knowing whether, in what I perceive to be my final hour, I'll cry out for assistance from some celestial being who I have every reason to believe doesn't exist. If I do, it won't make me a hypocrite — it'll just mean that I'm desperate. When you don't have anywhere to turn, it's only natural to start hoping against hope that someone — anyone — will care. And not just someone, but someone who can do something about the damned lousy mess you've gotten yourself into.

James Morrow, an author who considers himself a secular humanist, says the catchphrase "isn't an argument against atheists, it's an argument against foxholes."

He has a point.

A foxhole is a small pit soldiers dig for shelter in the midst of a raging battle. Without theism, we might have a lot fewer of them. How many foxholes were created because theists insist on fighting wars over whose god has the bigger cojones? Or which god's followers should have more land, loot and ladies? The incentives, however, go beyond the here and now. According to the hadith, a collection of sayings attributed to the prophet Muhammad, a martyr can look forward to six rewards:

1. Forgiveness "from the first moment his blood is spilled."
2. A seat in paradise.
3. Safety from the greatest terror — when the dead shall rise.
4. A crown from which a ruby is worth more than all the world.
5. Joining with seventy-two "wide-eyed maidens of paradise."
6. The ability to intercede for seventy-two relatives.

The rewards for Christians taking part in the first crusade of 1095 against the Muslims were slightly less elaborate but also compelling. Pope Urban II promised that "all who die by the way, whether by land or by sea, in the battle against the (Muslims), shall have immediate (forgiveness) of sins." It seems both sides have been known to distribute Get out of Jail Free cards as incentive for engaging in acts of war.

As they say, war is hell.

And soldiers are only human. Given the choice between life or death, the default is the former option. Survival mechanisms reinforced by evolution over millions of years demand that — all else being equal — we fight to stay alive using whatever methods we find at our disposal. If we're stuck in a foxhole or facing inoperable cancer, and we've exhausted all natural methods, it's only natural for us to hope against hope for something we haven't considered. Something outside our experience or even beyond what we might normally have believed in.

It's somewhat amusing that Darwinian principles should spur us to seek out divine intervention.

Sometimes, to be sure, all things are *not* equal. There are those who will give their lives willingly for a cause or another person, and this variable is precisely that religious leaders prey upon in sending soldiers overseas to fight holy wars. To overcome the natural survival instinct, they introduce the concept of the noble sacrifice. After all, didn't Jesus say that greater love has no man than this: that he lay down his life for his friends? Such noble self-sacrifice certainly has its place. For example, three men stepped in front of their girlfriends when a crazed shooter targeted the women in a Colorado movie theater just weeks before this book was written. That's heroism. Yet religious leaders have tapped this noble instinct time and again over the centuries to serve their own more selfish motives. When honorable self-sacrifice isn't enough to fan the flames of martyrdom, they seek to negate to will to survive by portraying this life as fleeting and despicable when compared to the joys available in the next. This is where the forgiveness of sins and the seventy-two maidens come into play.

Imagine a car dealer promises you can trade in your old Ford Taurus for a brand new Maserati with no money down and no questions asked. The only problem: He won't actually show you the car he's promising until you part with your current model. You have to take him at his word that it's in stock and that he will, in fact, carry out his end of the bargain once you've committed to the deal by handing him your keys.

You might hesitate at such an offer. What's the angle? Why is he holding out on me? What does he have to hide.

Even if it's on the level, it *sounds* too good to be true.

This is pretty much what religious leaders are saying when they throw out promises of rewards in the afterlife in exchange for your sacrifices in the here and now. True, your car will eventually give out in any case. If you fail to take the car dealer up on his offer of the Maserati, you'll be stuck without any transportation when that time eventually arrives. Yet if the car dealer is pulling a fast one — the old bait-and-switch — you'll be out of luck a lot sooner if you hand him the keys to your Taurus.

Soldiers who find themselves in foxholes have less choice in the matter than would-be recruits for some holy crusade. Their cars are running on empty already, so an entirely different dynamic is in play when that salesman suddenly appears beside them in the bunker. Now he's not some religious leader but merely an invisible presence, a voice in the back of their heads, prompting them to "Ask God (or Allah or Yawheh or Jesus) for help! What do you have to lose?"

Now, the salesman has you by the balls.

The cojones, if you will.

If you believe in a god who has the ability to save you from such sticky situations, you have to wonder about his ethics at this point. Those who live to tell the tale may gush about how the Almighty saved them from such a perilous predicament, simply because they pledged a newfound faith. Yet what about those who did the same and didn't live to tell the tale? The reports of foxhole conversions are necessarily skewed in favor of the converted, for the simple reason that those who pledged their fealty and were blown to kingdom come anyway can't be asked about it … and those who survived without asking for divine intervention aren't likely to talk about something that never happened.

Some believers question the value of such foxhole conversions in any case, pointing out with more than a little justification that the motives behind such confessions are suspect. It's the same sort of argument used, again with plenty of justification, by critics of torture. They argue that information extracted at the point of a knife — or by such methods as waterboarding — can be less than reliable. Intelligence gleaned through torture is hopelessly tainted because people are liable to say anything (most specifically, anything they believe their interrogator *wants* them to say) in order to stop the pain. Plenty of people, for instance, confessed to being witches when "put to the question" by the Inquisition, but it's highly doubtful that many of them actually engaged in witchcraft.

This is why courts refuse to recognize contracts signed under duress. They're thrown out of court as invalid.

Information obtained under torture is just as (un)reliable.

It's easy to focus on the person being questioned under threat or torture, but what of the questioner? Isn't such treatment, by its very nature, inhumane and sadistic? The United Nations, for one, has reached this very conclusion. It condemns torture under the following definition: "Any act by which severe pain or suffering, whether physical or mental, is intentionally inflicted on a person for such purposes as obtaining from him or a third person, information or a confession, punishing him for an act he or a third person has committed or is suspected of committing, or intimidating or coercing him or a third person, for any reason based on discrimination of any kind, when such pain or suffering is inflicted by or at the instigation of or with the consent or acquiescence of a public official or other person acting in an official capacity."

Although this is one of the worst examples of a run-on fragment sentence I've seen, this definition pretty much covers all the bases. Specifically, I'd like to draw the reader's attention to the last portion, which places responsibility on anyone acting in an official capacity who merely consents or acquiesces to the infliction of pain or suffering for the aforementioned purposes.

Perhaps you can see what I'm getting at here.

The soldier who makes a foxhole pledge of faith is doing so under circumstances that, to all intents and purposes, must feel very much like torture. Who is the person acting in an official capacity in such cases? The opposing army? Not really. The other side may be attempting to impose its will on our foxhole friend, but it has no official authority over him. Yet if one believes in an all-powerful God who is intimately concerned with the daily doings of humankind, one has to concede that such a deity constitutes someone acting in an official capacity. If, therefore, such a god consents or acquiesces to the continued infliction of torment upon a soldier hunkered down under enemy fire, one must conclude that this deity is engaging in a form of torture that has been roundly condemned by the United Nations.

Again, it seems, we humans are often more ethical than the gods we serve.

The Compassionate Instinct

The main difference between theist and non-theist morality, as noted earlier, is its point of origin. In its simplest terms, theists rely primarily on external directives from God or his appointed representative. Non-theists, on the other hand, rely first and foremost on their own consciences.

The natural assumption is that theists are more giving and compassionate toward their fellow human beings. Yet why should we assume this? Two reasons come to mind immediately, both based on theistic dogma. One involves the nature of human character. Christians, in particular, view humanity as intrinsically flawed or tainted by original sin. Following this point logically to its warped conclusion, they maintain with Paul that the entire race is captive to a sinful nature, having been "sold as a slave to sin" (Rom. 7:14). Humans, it seems, can't do anything right and therefore *must* rely on God for moral guidance. This position is taken not only in Paul's letters but also in the Qur'an, which states that "whatever good happens to you is from Allah, and whatever evil happens is from yourself" (4:79).

There's no evidence, empirical or historical, to support such absolutist folderol. Ascribing flaws in the human condition to a hypothetical event no one witnessed and for which there is no verifiable record is bad enough. Postulating that this event affected the rest of humanity like some genetic plague is worse. Ascribing all the good things that humanity undeniably does to an unseen, phantom being whose very existence remains unproven is perhaps the most absurd leap of the bunch.

The second assumption involves the nature of God. Because theists believe that God is absolutely good, it only makes sense for one to "go to the source" (as it were) in search of moral guidance. The problem with this assumption, as we've seen, is that an omnipotent creator is equally responsible for both good *and* evil, so it's a flip of the coin which sort of moral advice you're going to get. Turn the other cheek or wipe out the Amalekites? Forgive seventy times seven or wipe out virtually all your own creation by flooding the entire earth? Bless Job or afflict him? This is not the sort of fickle philosopher I want advising me on ethical decision-making.

With these assumptions off the table, it's time to propose an alternative hypothesis: Human beings are, in fact, better at making positive ethical choices on their own — without reference to a divine agent.

Why should this be so?

For starters, they're more efficient. They don't have to get the go-ahead from some outside source to act. The process suggested by Jesus — love your god and love your neighbor — is streamlined to simply the second half of this equation. The latter practice is commonly referred to as empathy, and a recent study supports the proposition those unencumbered by theism are better at it than those who act based on dogmatic decrees.

The research, conducted by a team from the University of California at Berkeley, was published in the journal *Social Psychology and Personality Science*. It found that nonreligious people were more likely than religious individuals to be motivated by compassion for their fellow human being.

Three studies were conducted. In the first, people were presented with various statements such as "When I see someone being taken advantage of, I feel kind of protective towards them." Those who agreed with such statements were more likely to engage in so-called random acts of kindness. This is significant because it shows how motivation works. Those who are motivated by an internal *feeling* of compassion are more likely to act on that feeling than those who don't have the same degree of empathy.

The second experiment found that less religious people were

more likely to be influenced by a video showing the effects of children on poverty. When given an opportunity to share money with a stranger in need, the least religious participants in the study were likely to give more. As with the first experiment, the results seem to indicate that the least religious people were the most likely to identify with others and, as an end result, to help them.

The final experiment found that feelings of compassion predicted greater levels of generosity among college students who were less religious. The same was not true, however, for more religious students.

Does this tell us that less religious people are somehow "better than" their more religious counterparts?

Not at all.

This isn't a commentary on intrinsic worth. It's a commentary on what works. This isn't a condemnation of religious people. In fact, the author holds a higher view of many religious folks than they hold of themselves. I certainly don't think they are slaves to sin. On the contrary, I think they're just as intrinsically capable of noble and honorable acts as anyone else. But when they put their faith in an external, hypothetical deity rather than in their own capacity for goodness, they add an element to their decision-making that can either impede or directly contradict their impulse for empathy.

Wisdom statements such as the golden rule affirm just such an impulse. On the other hand, the kind of dogma that reviles human nature as essentially "evil" suppresses it. If I'm incapable of anything truly good, why should I trust my own feelings when they tell me to reach out and help someone else? This need for a second opinion, intrinsic in the dogma of Western monotheism, indicates a lack of trust in one's own ability to make moral decisions.

The focus therefore shifts from the need for compassion to the need for affirmation. The theist is distracted from the need in front of his face — the child in poverty or the person being abused — because he has turned his attention to the heavens, seeking divine validation for his own compassion. What does this say about a theist who sees a train approaching a man on the railroad tracks? Is he less likely to make a split-second decision to rush forward and push the man out of harm's way? There's no indication of this. In times of crisis, when immediate action is needed to avert catastrophe, the theist has no time to check with his divine master on whether his action is dogmatically correct. He won't have time to ask whether the man on the tracks is gay or straight, a veteran or a civilian, a saint or a mass murderer, a Democrat or a Republican. In times such as these, he's likely to follow his own internal instincts.

It's during times which afford the opportunity for reflection that he's likely to sublimate his own compassion to what he has identified as "the will of God." That's the time when such a person can become truly dangerous.

Holy War and Rumors of War

Is compassion always a good thing?

To answer this question, we should perhaps return to the foxhole — or, more broadly to the battlefield.

Some might argue that compassion simply isn't appropriate in wartime. An effective military campaign can call for immediate and unquestioning obedience to one's superiors. They develop the strategy and call the shots. The soldiers on the front lines have a simple duty: carry out that strategy by following orders. This simple set-up maximizes efficiency. If soldiers were continually questioning orders, the chain of command would break down and nothing would get done. Accordingly, recruits are brought into boot camp and conditioned to follow orders without question. This could mean scrubbing the latrine with a toothbrush or standing at attention for hours on end. It could involve imitating Sisyphus by pushing rocks up a hill, then rolling them back down and repeating the process ad nauseam. It doesn't matter whether there's a point to any of this or not. What matters is pure, unquestioning obedience.

Exercises such as this are necessary to prepare the soldier for more difficult assignments, such as blowing the enemy's brains out on the battlefield at a single word from his commanding officer. Hesitation could be fatal … to the individual or, more importantly, to the mission. In war, the highest act of heroism is giving one's life for the cause, but the goal is exactly the opposite: taking another person's life for the very same reason.

There's no place for the golden rule in the heat of battle. There's no room for a soldier to consider how he'd like to be treated, and there's even less room for treating someone on the other side according to that standard. That whole bit about loving your enemies and praying for those who persecute you? Forget about it. The enemy is to be objectified to the greatest extent possible. They're not fellow human beings. They're Gooks or Japs or Krauts or Nips. Such offensive labels accomplish two things — they dehumanize the enemy and lump them all into a single category. You're not attacking individuals, but "the enemy" in some singular sense. It's a black-and-white world very similar to the sort of world imagined by fundamentalist religious groups.

It should come as no surprise that these latter often view the world in terms of what they call "spiritual warfare." They latch on to the imagery of Ephesians 6, which describes the believer's struggle in militaristic terms. The reader is invited to don the armor of God, the breastplate of righteousness, the belt of truth, the shield of faith and the helmet of salvation. Such vivid and visual metaphors, often prominently featured in sermons, reveal nothing more clearly than a deeply ingrained attitude of defensiveness. The enemies in this struggle are described categorically as "evil." Once you've placed this label on the enemy, compassion is no longer an option.

Just ask the early church father Origen Adamantius, who dared to postulate that all beings could be reconciled with God … even Satan. Orthodox leaders were so troubled by this prospect that they published a list of fifteen anathemas against Origen some three centuries after his death. Among them were these last two:

1. If anyone says or thinks that the power of God is limited, and that he created as much as he was able to compass, let him be anathema!"

2. If anyone says or believes that the punishment of demons and impious men is only temporary, and will one day have an end, and that restoration will take place of demons and impious men, let him be anathema!"

The juxtaposition of these two statements, one right after the other, constitutes the height of absurdity. The first condemns the idea of a limited God; the second proclaims that this unlimited god either can't or won't show compassion toward those who have offended him. The first anathema puts "can't" off the table. And to believe that such a god "won't" show compassion toward those who have offended him violates not only the teachings of Jesus concerning forgiveness but also biblical description of his very nature as a god of love.

They have, in effect, exchanged the god of love so often referenced by Jesus for the god of war whose fingerprints are all over the Old Testament and who was resurrected in an even more hideously cruel form by Paul. (As the reader may have guessed, I'm not a particular fan of Paul's writings, but I won't demonize him, either; his summation of love in his first letter to the Corinthians stands as among the most poetic and inspiring passages in any volume of scripture.)

This war god is a god who demonizes and dehumanizes "the others." All the better to persecute them mercilessly, condemn them and burn them — either at the stake or in a contrived eternal torture chamber — without even the slightest twinge of guilt. Employing this military mindset on the battlefield has led to atrocities ranging from the slaughter of Jericho and Ai in the Book of Joshua to the 16th century St. Bartholomew's Day massacre of the Huguenots in Paris; from Odessa and Warsaw to Wounded Knee and My Lai. Employing it off the battlefield is even more common, and sometimes more deadly. It has led to concentration camps, brutal repression and ethnic cleansing.

This is the price we pay for a mindset that suppresses compassion and rewards self-righteous anger. Perhaps this is necessary in war. Perhaps it is one of those so-called "necessary evils." But perhaps we should not be asking ourselves whether compassion has any place on the battlefield. Perhaps we should instead be asking whether battlefields would have any place in our world if we exercised more compassion. If the belief in a god who encourages us to place obedience above our sense of empathy inhibits our ability to care about others, what does that tell us about that god? Or about our decision to follow him?

Are we, in the end, itching for a fight?

And if so, what does it say about the dedication of Jesus' followers to his core teachings about conflict?

If you are placing something on the altar and remember that your neighbor has something against you, do not offer up your sacrifice until you have first reconciled with your neighbor. Settle matters with your adversary before the case gets to court. Do not let anger rise up against your brother or sister. The one who lives by the sword shall die by it.

It is difficult to see how such teachings can be reconciled with the bloodthirsty attitude that pervades so many supposedly Christian teachings. It is not at all hard, however, to understand why Christianity, as so often practiced today, suffers from severe credibility issues among thinking people beyond the confines of the church.

Some Christians, especially the evangelical sort, seem to veritably salivate over the prospect of Armageddon, a climactic battle between good and evil that's supposed to take place in the Middle East. Fire-and-brimstone preachers let their voices reach an almost orgasmic crescendo as they exult in the drama of this hypothetical battle that will, they are quite sure, result in ultimate victory for their side. The Beast who brands his followers with the number 666 (or 616, depending on the translation). That nasty ol' dragon. The angels and their seven trumpets. The four horsemen of the apocalypse, who usher in pestilence, famine, war and death.

Their sermons, reinforced by pop culture references and portrayals, have succeeded in searing such imagery into our cultural consciousness so successfully that a Time/CNN poll taken in the early years of this new millennium found that 59 percent of Americans believed that the events depicted in the Book of Revelation would come to pass at some future date.

When one realizes that the book of Revelation, upon which the entire scenario is based, was meant as an indictment of the Emperor Nero, one has to feel just a little silly at the idea of this book foretelling the future. The name Nron Qsr, in Greek, has a numerical value of 666, while the variant Nro Qsr carries a value of 616. Nero was almost certainly dead by the time the book was written, but independent historians of the era tell us rumors were circulating that he was still alive. Nero was Elvis before Elvis was Elvis. No one was quite sure whether he had really left the building.

The well-known identification of the "Babylon" mentioned in the text with Rome only strengthens this association. In the final analysis, associating the so-called antichrist with some modern figure is about as sensible as identifying a man named Jesus with a figure from prophecy known as Immanuel who was supposed to have been born several centuries earlier. One can try to force incompatible puzzle pieces together, but the pieces will wind up broken and the resulting image will be distorted at best, unrecognizable at worst.

And they certainly don't justify the thirst for conflict that seems to follow monotheism around like an unholy shadow.

"If the obstacles of bigotry and priestcraft can be surmounted, we may hope that common sense will suffice to do everything else."

— Thomas Jefferson

Fifteen: The Chosen Ones

One of the most peculiar elements of the "warrior Christianity" that supplanted Jesus' gospel of peace is its treatment of the Jews.

To call it a love-hate relationship would be to put it mildly.

For centuries, Christians used various verses from the gospels, taken out of context, as a pretext for hatred of the entire Jewish people. The Jews as a whole were blamed for rejecting Jesus as their rightful messiah, and a mob of Jews was quoted as calling directly for his crucifixion with a curse they supposedly laid upon themselves in perpetuity: "His blood be upon us and our children." Here is yet another affront to the concepts of justice and individual responsibility — one more instance during which succeeding generations are made to pay for the supposed sins of the fathers.

This is the very essence of bigotry.

There was even the notion that identified Judas, "the betrayer," with the Jews as a whole, based on the association of his Hebrew name (Judah) with the tribe that gave its name to the Jewish nation. By this sort of reasoning, if a mass murderer turned out to be named Christian, one could justifiably use this as a basis to condemn all

Christians and their children. The sheer idiocy of such thinking should be self-evident.

Idiocy, however, has always seemed to find a place in fundamentalist religions, and it often turns out to be deadly. Long before Nazi Germany condemned millions of Jews to death in gas chambers and forced labor camps, Jews were being persecuted, exiled and murdered for their faith and ethnic identity. Jews were blamed for the Black Death in Europe and burned alive by the hundreds. In the late 13th century, the Edict of Expulsion banned all Jews from England. In the Papal States, under the direct rule of the pope Jews were allowed to remain but were confined to ghettos and required to attend sermons urging them to convert to Christianity.

After World War II, however, something happened to shift the balance. Hitler's so-called final solution was turned on its head, and thousands of Jews fled Germany and the other states under Nazi control for their ancestral homeland. The arrival of roughly a quarter of a million Jews made them a substantial, though still minority, portion of the population in a territory that had long been predominantly Arab and Muslim in character. With no prospect for returning to their former homes, many Jews set down roots and called upon family members to join them in what had once been — and had now again become — their "promised" land. In essence, the biblical invasion of Palestine that was said to have occurred under Joshua was being repeated, and once again the people who were living there at the time became displaced. In 1950, two years after the state of Israel was established, the United Nations counted nearly three-quarters of a million Palestinian refugees.

Considering their past antipathy toward the Jews, one might have expected the Christian masses to side with the Palestinians. Two factors, however, mitigated against this. The first was the simple fact that most Europeans had no interest in reintegrating the Jews into their communities. As long as they were in Israel, they were somebody else's problem. Europeans nations were in the midst of rebuilding from a devastating conflict that had left millions dead and cities in ruin. They had no resource to offer the Jews. But the second factor had nothing to do with Europe and everything to do with evangelical Christians in the United States.

Evangelical leaders had found evidence that the birth of Israel in 1948 marked a key fulfillment of Old Testament prophecy that would usher in the "end times" (cue spooky and ominous soundtrack music).

Had not the prophet Amos predicted, "I will bring back my exiled people Israel. They shall rebuild the ruined cities and live in them"? Had not Ezekiel declared that the Jews would return to the land of their ancestors, where they would become one nation under a single king? And the prophet Isaiah, had he not foretold that God would gather his people to Judah from the four corners of the Earth?

Suddenly, the Jews had gone from "Christ killers" back to being "God's chosen people." It was a peculiar transformation, to say the least, but it was consistent with that nettlesome tendency of monotheists to view the world in stark, two-dimensional terms. For hundreds of years, the Jews had been persecuted as evil incarnate; now, abruptly, they had become a privileged class to be fawned over. All this really demonstrates, however, is that truth is seldom found at the extremes. The Jews as a people were no more responsible for Jesus' death than all Brits were responsible for the beheading of Anne Boleyn. The parallel? Both the "king of the Jews" and the queen of England were executed on a trumped-up charge of treason. Similarly, the founding of the state of Israel has nothing to do with the "end times," which — if we are to believe the Book of Revelation — should have occurred during the second half of the first century CE. Nonetheless, the United States has used this so-called prophecy as justification for supporting Israel virtually without question in its conflict with the Palestinian people. There are, to be sure, practical considerations. Israel holds a strategic position as a key U.S. ally in a particularly volatile corner of the world. Yet this is not the reason given by evangelicals for supporting the Jewish state.

Conservative Christian pastor John Hagee not only characterized the support of Israel as "God's foreign policy," he further stated that evangelical Christians are "on the front line of defense for Israel in the United States of America." These sentiments were voiced by a man who has (in print, no less) compared a woman with PMS to a snarling Doberman pinscher.

One might be tempted to dismiss Hagee's rhetoric on the grounds that such bigotry operates on the fringes of society, yet this is a man whose San Antonio megachurch has been ranked among the forty biggest in the country, with an average attendance of 10,000 people. His influence was such that he endorsed John McCain for president in 2008 to great fanfare before his controversial remarks caused McCain to repudiate Hagee's support.

It would be one thing if Hagee were the only person to express such views regarding Israel, but he's not. Evangelical Christian leaders from across the spectrum have counseled support for Israel regardless of that nation's actions or policies. Southern Baptist leader Richard Land explained the rationale in the following terms: "American evangelicals have it in their DNA: God blesses those who bless the Jews and curses whoever curses the Jews." So there you have it. Once again, morality isn't based on action, but rather on ethnic identity. The Nazis killed the Jews because of who they were; now evangelical Christians in America are exalting them for the very same reason. Not because of the quality of their character, but because of their genes. This is, unfortunately, a recurring theme.

Land's position becomes even more troubling when one considers his post within the Southern Baptist Convention: He has served for nearly a quarter-century as president of the group's "ethics and religious liberty commission."

Ethics.

Now *that's* scary.

What, precisely, is ethical about grabbing onto the coattails of "Gods' chosen people" for the purely selfish motive of ensuring God's continued blessing upon your own country? Excuse me, but this is somehow ethical? I don't think so. In fact, if I were in Israel's position, that would be cause for not only offense but concern. If the United States is simply supporting Israel because it's theologically convenient, it doesn't say much for the moral underpinnings of such support. What happens, for instance, when American Christian conservatives discover that their premise is incorrect. God hasn't, by any stretch of the imagination, blessed those who bless the Jews and curse those who curse them. The Catholic Church became the wealthiest institution on the face of the planet while condemning the Jews as Christ killers. Tell me exactly how this fits into the American evangelical's formula of cause and effect.

Divine Rights … and Wrongs

This is the fundamental difficulty with designating any people the "chosen ones." Once special status is conferred based on identity rather than action, one is pretty much free to ignore morality altogether. In a society built on genetics rather than ethics, there's simply no motivation to uphold any particular set of ethical principles. This is true of any model that emphasizes bloodlines over character and achievement.

Supposed genetic superiority is the principle behind concepts ranging from the Indian caste system to Aryan supremacy to the identification of Israel as a chosen people. It can be found in ethnocentric systems the world over, and its motivation is always the same: assert rights based on an artificially static reality and a sense of entitlement, rather than recognizing hard work, achievement and adaptability in the face of continual change.

European monarchs justified their often corrupt and incompetent reigns by invoking the so-called "divine right of kings." According to this doctrine, monarchs derived their right to rule directly from God; in consequence, they were not subject to any earthly authority. The abuse inherent in this system gave rise to revolts such as the one that led to Britain's adoption of the Magna Carta, along with the French and American Revolutions.

Reacting to the abuses of a "divinely installed" monarch, George III, the architects of the U.S. system installed a series of checks and balances to ensure that no one branch of government could exercise absolute authority over any other. This prudent precaution, however, didn't keep Americans from repeatedly trying to assert their pre-eminence and promote their own identity as a chosen nation. Alexis de Tocqueville coined the term "American exceptionalism" in the early 19th century to describe this inclination. Evidence of it can be found in such phrases as "my country right or wrong" — again emphasizing identity over ethics — and "manifest destiny," a doctrine used to justify American expansion across the continent at the expense of indigenous people. I'm sure the Cherokee, Cheyenne, Lakota Sioux, Apache, Comanche and other Native American nations must not have subscribed to this line of "reasoning."

Chickens and Eggs

Human beings, it should be said, don't need some scriptural or priestly sanction to behave badly, any more than they are dependent on divine power to perform acts of virtue. Tyranny, enslavement and all their attendant horrors can be performed quite effectively without reference to a heavenly mandate. The Soviet Union under Josef Stalin, for example, was officially an atheist state. Under his rule, at least 36 million people behind what came to be known as the Iron Curtain were executed. Millions more were deported or sent into exile, while nearly 20 million passed through a system of more than fifty Gulag labor camps — many of them north of the Arctic Circle in Siberia — and more than four hundred labor colonies during Stalin's reign of terror.

Stalin didn't need a god's authority to engage in the wave of atrocities. In fact, he once scoffed at the pope, asking, "How many divisions does he have?"

Yet Stalin's methods were remarkably similar to those of the militant theocrat. The state took on the role of a pseudo-deity by the name of Mother Russia. Stalin became the savior, with cities renamed in his honor and statues erected in city squares. The same treatment was accorded to his predecessor, Vladimir Lenin, whose body was embalmed and placed on public display at a mausoleum specifically designed for this purpose. The tomb became a sort of holy relic and a destination for pilgrims from across Russia to pay their respects.

Stalin and his fellows may have claimed atheism, but it was merely the wilted rose of theocracy called by another name. The same could be said of the fascist regime in Italy under Benito Mussolini, who flatly declared that "fascism is a religion" and "the 20th century will be known in history as the century of fascism."

What does this prove?

Not that god exists, or that he doesn't as any sort of independent entity. Merely that humans motivated to control and enslave others will resort to tried-and-true methods time after time — not because they're condoned or condemned by some deity, but for a much simpler reason.

They work.

Men like Stalin and Mao Zedong ordered the massacre of millions while spurning any explicit reference to something called "god." The writers of the Hebrew Bible and the medieval popes used just such references to justify similar behavior. The results, in all instances, were precisely the same: brutality, displacement, mass murder.

The presence of a deity, per se, appears to be entirely irrelevant when seeking an explanation of human cruelty. Some tyrants appeal to heaven as a means of justifying their atrocities, but others think it needless to fabricate such approval and plunge ahead with their vile acts regardless. This would appear to let God off the hook.

But if God is not a factor in human behavior when it comes to cruelty, one must ask whether he plays any part in *positive* human behavior. As the Josephson Institute study showed, the belief in God doesn't seem to make much difference there, either. It appears that humanity, not deity, is the deciding factor — and therefore, the point of origin — for good deeds as well as vile acts. The upshot of this is that we may well have gotten it all backwards. To borrow the words inscribed on the back of Jethro Tull's 1971 album *Aqualung*, "In the beginning Man created God; and in the image of Man created he him. And Man gave unto God a multitude of names, that he might be Lord of all the earth when it was suited to Man."

It would seem that people bent on cruelty create gods in their own image, rather than the other way around. And, one can only hope that people disposed toward compassion create gods in their own image, too.

At least this last bit of information should be taken as encouraging.

Unfortunately for the orthodox Christian, he can't accept it. He can't even consider the possibility of humans creating a compassionate god — not merely because he can't stomach the idea of a human creator, but also because his dogma leaves no room for human-based compassion. All good things must come from God. One could, conceivably, condemn the biblical instances of genocide, murder, pillage and the like as being no different than the sort of thing practiced by Stalin. There would be biblical precedent for this, straight from the mouth of Jesus: "By their fruit you will recognize them. Do people pick grapes from briars or figs from thistles? Likewise, every good tree bears good fruit, but a bad tree produces bad fruit" (Matt. 7:16-17).

Tyranny? Repression? Murder?

Bad fruit.

The only possible conclusion, then is that those who practice such things constitute a bad tree, whether they they're named Joseph (Stalin) or Joshua (son of Nun). But this conclusion, sadly, is also unacceptable to the Bible-believing theist, who finds the teachings of his savior directly at odds with the supposed directives of his god. Even the Christian apologist C.S. Lewis saw the fundamental problem of such contradictory claims: "It is no more possible for God than for the weakest of his creatures to carry out both of two mutually exclusive alternatives; not because his power meets an obstacle, but because nonsense remains nonsense even when we talk it about God."

And that's precisely what we're left with when we strip away the dross and boil everything down to its simplest form.

Nonsense.

Contradiction — or hypocrisy, to use the term Jesus employed in rebuking the Pharisees — is fatal to the cause of credibility. Defending himself against the charge of demonic possession, Jesus declared that a kingdom divided against itself could not stand. He was speaking of the kingdom of Satan, but the principle applies equally to the kingdom of God. Replace the word "Satan" with "God" in his teaching on the subject, and it still rings just as true: "If God drives out God, how then can his kingdom endure?"

When Abraham Lincoln was faced with a nation at war against himself, he recognized the same fundamental principle. In his second inaugural address, referencing a civil war that cost more than 600,000 men their lives, he said: "In great contests, each party claims to act in accordance with the will of God. Both *may* be, and one *must* be wrong. God cannot be *for* and *against* the same thing at the same time."

Or, alternatively, the two claims simply cancel each other out, leaving us with a god who isn't the least bit interested in petty human conflicts but, in fact, has much better things to do with his time. Such a god is a disinterested deity who has no stake in human politics, much as we have no particular interest in the politics of a beehive or an anthill. Why is it so frightening to consider the possibility that we are, in fact, masters of our own destiny? That it's not written in the stars or decreed in ancient scripture or laid out before us as some predetermined course that leads us inexorably toward salvation on the one hand or damnation on the other?

Could it be that we're simply lazy and a trifle insecure?

We want a god to fight our war for us, or at the very least affirm our right to declare them. We want a god who can serve as a safety net when we're out of options, facing a terminal illness or stuck in a foxhole with no apparent avenue for escape. We want a god who can guarantee that things will always be just the way they are; whether we're comfortably ensconced in a penthouse suite or comfortably numb to the abuse inflicted against us. Either way, we can deal with it, as long as we don't have to change.

We want to be the chosen people. We want a god who can make us feel important and special — more important than those ignoramuses who are somehow different because of their skin color or economic status or language or sexual orientation. We want a god who will protect us from them, lest they inflict their differentness upon us. And, of course, we want a god who will grant us everlasting life in an eternal paradise free from the irksome upheavals that plague and typify our present existence.

Yet defining gods in terms of our own psychological needs makes them little more than projections of our own neuroses and wishful thinking. It does them a far greater disservice than the sort of questions posed by Job or the modern skeptic. It also creates in us a tendency to worship our own fears as though they were all-powerful; and, perhaps worst of all, it leads us to inflict those fears on others in an attempt to validate our own skewed view of the divine.

In the movie *Dogma*, a "thirteenth apostle" named Rufus — excised from the biblical narrative because of his skin color — waxes philosophical about the nature of God in a conversation with Bethany, the film's protagonist.

"He still digs humanity," Rufus tells Bethany, "but it bothers him to see the shit that gets carried out in his name — wars, bigotry, televangelism — but especially all the factioning of all the religions. He said humanity took a good idea and, like always, built a belief structure on it."

"Having beliefs isn't good?" Bethany asks.

"I think it's better to have ideas," Rufus tells her. "You can change an idea. Changing a belief is trickier."

So it is.

"If a black cat crosses your path, it signifies that the animal is going somewhere."

— Groucho Marx

Sixteen: Black Cat-astrophes

Step on a crack, break your mother's back.

I can remember walking along the sidewalk to school, not believing that such a thing would ever happen, but nonetheless avoiding cracks. I saw it as a challenge, and if I happened to misstep here and there, I shrugged it off. By the time I got home that afternoon to find my mother's spine mercifully intact, I had forgotten all about the sing-song voice that had played idly at the back of my consciousness that morning.

Superstition, however, isn't always so harmless.

During the Middle Ages, many Europeans believed that cats were the agents of Satan. They were independent little creatures, often skulking about in the shadows, and their reflective eyes gave off an eerie glow when the light caught them just right. Their loud wailing during mating added to their "evil" mystique. The church itself either created or encouraged this fear when Pope Gregory IX proclaimed that a heretical sect in southern France had been discovered worshiping the devil … in the form of a black cat.

By the time the bubonic plague arrived more than a century later, the superstition was so deeply ingrained in the populace that the cats were natural scapegoats. Believing the felines were to blame for bringing the plague down upon them, the superstitious commoners started killing the animals by the thousands. This ultimately proved to be their undoing. The cats, it turned out, were not carriers of the plague at all. Quite to the contrary: The true carriers were rats that had been infected by flea bites. Had the Europeans protected the cats instead of eradicating them, the cats would have protected *them* in turn … by killing or chasing away the rats.

The misguided campaign of cruelty toward felines shows how hard it is to distinguish faith from superstition. Complicating matters is the role that fear plays in both these systems of belief. The philosopher Bertrand Russell remarked that "fear is the main source of superstition, and one of the main sources of cruelty." No doubt the dear departed cats would attest to that on both counts. "To conquer fear," Russell continued, "is the beginning of wisdom."

Compare this to a saying repeated more than once in the Old Testament: "The fear of the Lord is the beginning of wisdom."

The reader can judge which philosophy is the more prudent.

The Europeans would have been wise to conquer their irrational fear of cats, yet they refused to do so. There was certainly good reason to fear the plague, but there was no reason at all to fear the cats who might have protected them. Killing cats in this instance was no better than offering up animal sacrifices to propitiate the gods — be they god of the Old Testament with his fatted calves and Passover lambs or the so-called "heathen" gods of the surrounding city-states. And it was no more effective.

In fact, given the cats' talent for chasing off rodents, it was even less so. Even when the Europeans identified fleas as the source of the scourge, they failed to call off their deadly campaign against the felines. On the contrary, they redoubled their efforts to eradicate the cats under the false impression that these animals were the ones carrying the infected fleas. In some places, owning a cat was outlawed, and the English killed so many cats that they nearly rid the island of them altogether. Black cats were seen as especially bad.

Over time, the bias against black cats become so deeply ingrained in Western culture that the image of such an animal crossing one's path persisted as a supposed augur of ill fortune. (Fortunately, however, reports of abusive activities involving black cats at Halloween appear to be largely an urban myth).

The Hammer of the Witches

By the time the Black Plague had run its course, one-third or more of Europe's human population had succumbed to the plague. Millions of cats had been burned along with them, but that wasn't even the worst of it. The panic set in motion by the so-called "fear of the Lord" also claimed the lives of tens or even hundreds of thousands of individuals accused of witchcraft. As with the terror involving the cats, the church fanned the flames of anxiety concerning those accused of consorting with Satan. The Catholic Church even went so far as to commission a work by a pair of Inquisitors specifically condemning witches. Known as the *Malleus Maleficarum* or *Hammer of the Witches*, it contained specific instructions for dealing with accused witches — how to conduct their trials, how to employ various methods of torture in questioning them, and how to "prove" their supposed guilt.

Interestingly, this document — which appeared in no fewer than 29 editions — admits that God himself must grant permission for witchcraft to occur. This would hardly seem to be the act of a "good" god, or even a sensible one. It is, however, fully consistent with the portrayal of a deity who hardens people's hearts in order to prolong the agony rather than cutting to the chase.

The lengths that believers will go to in their desire to rationalize this sort of irrational behavior seldom cease to amaze me. Joni Eareckson Tada, an evangelical author who suffered a diving accident that left her a quadriplegic, has written that "sometimes God allows what he hates (in order) to accomplish what he loves." This is supposed to be inspirational. Yet it's hard to distinguish between this sentiment and more (in)famous statement of Niccolo Machiavelli: "The ends justify the means."

Is God to be credited with the same sort of cutthroat policies advocated by this medieval philosopher? That would, perhaps, be too generous. In too many cases, the Judeo-Christian God is not depicted as sacrificing his ethics because he finds it necessary in order to achieve some noble goal. Rather, he's shown sacrificing his ethics when it is entirely unnecessary — or even counterproductive — to do so.

He is omnipotent, after all.

This is not to pick on Tada. Her ability to triumph in the face of severe adversity is a testament to her own perseverance and positive outlook. Rather than painting a positive picture of her god, however, her reaction exposes him as a Machiavellian sadist who exhibits signs of Dissociative Identity Disorder, allowing what he hates in order to accomplish what he loves when such a convoluted process isn't at all necessary. The picture that emerges is one of a heavenly trickster who is toying with Tada — and the rest of us: a god who seems to have much more in common with the fickle Loki or wily Coyote than a beneficent and loving god.

Beneficence and love are certainly not qualities anyone would associate with the *Malleus Maleficarum*. The document seems, in places, to be nothing less than a guidebook for torture that could have been written by the Marquis de Sade. Consider the following excerpt:

"The method of beginning an examination by torture is as follows: First, the jailers prepare the implements of torture, then they strip the prisoner. ... And when the implements of torture have been prepared, the judge ... tries to persuade the prisoner to confess the truth freely; but, if he will not confess, he bid attendants make the prisoner fast to the strappado or some other implement of torture."

The strappado was sometimes called "reverse hanging." It was a means of torture in which the hands of the accused were tied behind the back. The Inquisitor would then attach a rope at the place where the wrists were bound and use a pulley to hoist the person entirely up off the ground. The weight of the body, sometimes augmented by additional dead weight, dislocated the person's arms, resulting in intense pain and sometimes even leading to paralysis.

Other means of torture were also used to "test" for witchcraft. Suspected witches were sometimes subjected to a trial by ordeal, in which they bound hand and foot before being deposited in a body of water. The trial? If they floated, they were guilty of witchcraft. If they sank to the bottom (and drowned!), they were innocent. Talk about a no-win situation. A variation on this method of torture involved a so-called ducking stool, a chair to which the woman was tied and which was then repeatedly immersed in water until she confessed to being a witch. Giles Corey, a man accused of witchcraft during the infamous Salem Trials of 1692, refused to enter a plea and was subsequently stripped naked, placed on a flat board and crushed to death beneath a succession of heavy stones, applied one at a time.

This is the kind of perverse sadism that arose as a result of church-sanctioned superstition. It would be a mistake to conclude that the church condemned those accused of witchcraft because of some disdain for superstitious practices. On the contrary, the church fully believed in the efficacy of the supposed witchcraft. Whereas the church condemned heretics because it believed their doctrines to be *false*, they condemned accused witches because they believed the accusations to be *true*. They believed the so-called witches' power to be real … or at least this was the official line. It certainly was convincing enough for the masses who were easily worked up into a frenzy whenever such accusations were made. But as to the church authorities themselves, it's entirely unclear whether they believed their own rhetoric. Hanging "witches" in public squares or burning them at the stake had the convenient effect of reinforcing the church's authority over "the devil" in a way that must have left quite an impression. On the one hand, it encouraged the faithful to remain secure in the knowledge that the church was in control. On the other, it encouraged these same faithful to *remain* faithful ... lest they be summarily accused and suffer the same fate.

Power does, indeed, corrupt. And the power to control the masses by fanning the flames of superstition should not be taken lightly.

One might wish that such church-sponsored paranoia had been consigned to the distant past. But less than a year before this writing, Pope Benedict XVI traveled to Africa with a message condemning the practice of witchcraft. The danger, he said, was real. Yet he was either unable or unwilling to acknowledge that the danger lay not in those accused of practicing witchcraft, but in their actions of their accusers.

Michael Katola, a lecturer on theology at the Catholic-affiliated Maryknoll Institute in Kenya, used language that could have been culled from medieval Europe in describing the situation in Africa: "Witchcraft is a reality," he declared. "It is not a superstition. Many communities know these powers exist. ... If we don't believe in the existence of witchcraft as Satanism, then we cannot deal with it."

Yet just as it was in Salem and elsewhere, it is precisely this mistaken belief that is causing the problem.

Three years before the pope's visit, Amnesty International reported that 1,000 accused witches in Gambia had been abducted by government-sponsored "witch doctors." A year earlier, four suspected witches were murdered in Burundi. A United Nations watchdog has reported that "violence against children accused of witchcraft is increasing, and children are being kept as prisoners in religious buildings where they are exposed to torture and ill-treatment or even killed under the pretext of exorcism."

In Ghana, accused witches are expelled from their homes and forced to live as exiles in "witch villages." At least six such villages exist in the West African country. The women who live there must deal with unsanitary conditions and abusive behavior by the men who run the camps. It's a life sentence. The women can never return home — even if they are exonerated — because the scarlet letter attached to the original accusation brands them, metaphorically, for life. Conditions are similar to those found in a refugee camp, and they find themselves at the mercy of overseers who use them as forced labor or sex slaves.

One woman reported being found guilty based solely on a shamanic ritual involving a mixture of gin and the blood of a chicken.

And this, according to the church, is not superstition?

Such a statement boggles the mind.

The Catholic Church, however, is far from the sole bastion of superstitious bigotry in the modern world. Accusations of witchcraft and Satanism have been leveled occasionally at various people in cases that seem to echo the hysteria present in the Salem Witch Trials. The operators of a day care in Manhattan Beach, Calif., stood accused of abusing 360 children in a case that included references to witchcraft. The seven-year trial became the most expensive criminal prosecution in U.S. history. In the end, all the charges were dropped.

Shortly before that case, a book titled *Michelle Remembers* was written in the style of an autobiography of a psychiatric patient who claimed to have recovered "repressed memories" of Satanic ritual abuse. The book has been largely discredited, with no evidence ever having been produced to corroborate the author's story. In the meantime, however, she secured a $100,000 advance for the hardcover version of the book, an additional $242,000 for paperback rights, and an option to make the whole thing into a movie.

A case in Kern County, also in California, led to the conviction of two couples during the 1980s, but those convictions were subsequently overturned. Six other accusations in the same county followed, but various cases fell apart and convictions were thrown out as accusers recanted their testimony.

It should be noted that members of some modern belief systems *do* claim to practice witchcraft, yet virtually all of them forcefully repudiate any connection with the worship of Satan. The following statement from the religioustolerance.org website typifies the response of most such practitioners, some of who practice a belief system known as Wicca: "Wiccans believe that they worship neither the Christian God nor the Christian devil. They worship a Goddess and a God. Neither is at all similar to Satan. Wicca, and other forms of Neopaganism, are as different from Satanism as Hinduism is from Chistianity."

As for cats, they're still damned good at chasing away dirty rats. Maybe we'll remember that the next time we're tempted to choose a scapegoat. Judging from their popularity on the social networking site Facebook, it seems at least we've learned *that* lesson.

"Two things are infinite: the universe and human stupidity; and I'm not sure about the universe."

— Albert Einstein

Seventeen: Flat-Earth Echoes

One of the most popular and tenacious arguments for the existence of God is the so-called First Cause argument. Beginning with the law of cause and effect, it postulates that something must have set the entire process in motion.

That "something" is, of course, identified as God.

The twin assumptions that undergird this reasoning are that the universe is both finite and linear. Assuming it's finite, it must therefore have a beginning and a conclusion, much like a book containing historical records. This first assumption leads to the second: reliance upon a linear model. The problem is, we don't have any basis for assuming the universe is finite — and we most likely never will. There's simply no way to test this hypothesis, unless and until we come to the "end" of the universe … assuming we would recognize such a thing when we saw it. What would it look like? An place devoid of stars? A place where "there be dragons"? The Great Wall of China on a celestial level?

Since we have no point of reference to recognize "nothingness," it's entirely possible that we'd miss it if it were right in front of our noses. How does one measure … nothing?

On the one hand, we have no way of recognizing such a limit to our "reality." On the other, it is literally impossible for a being with finite senses and limited perception to observe something limitless and confirm that it is, in fact, infinite.

Faced with these constraints, the theist throws up his hands and simply assumes that reality is finite.

Interesting.

Why doesn't the theist do the same when confronted with the concept of an infinite god? Why is it acceptable to affirm the existence of a limitless deity, yet unacceptable to admit the possibility of a limitless universe? The two hypotheses are equally unverifiable by finite human beings. Neither can be subjected to any sort of empirical testing, and both must therefore be accorded the exact same level of credibility.

In both cases, the answer is, "We don't know."

Or, rather, "We *can't* know."

We could attempt to infer an answer from what we do know, but such an inference would be speculative at best, and similar speculations have gotten us into trouble in the past. When talking about a line of cause and effect, we're speaking in temporal terms. One event leads to another, which in turn spawns another, and so forth. Indeed, one couldn't even speak of time in any meaningful sense without changes to mark how this moment is different than the previous one. When we string them all together, they form a linear succession — such is the simplistic model we employ.

All this is quite abstract, so let's bring things back down to earth (so to speak) by transferring our linear model to a spatial context. Most ancient cultures believed the world was flat. The Greek philosopher Thales thought it floated in the water like a log. Anaximander believed it was a cylinder with a flat top. Buddhists and others viewed it as a disk surrounded by mountains, while others adopted a similar model with water at the margins. The Chinese thought the world was flat and square. Astronomy eventually proved them all wrong. What appeared from a limited perspective to be a flat, linear model was in fact just a small segment of a much larger reality that turned out to be three-dimensional and spherical. If one walked the horizon in a straight line long enough, one would wind up right back at the "beginning" … no matter which location he chose as the starting point for his journey. The "straight line," in the final analysis, wasn't a line at all.

What if time operates in the same fashion? Our perspective on it is limited in much the same way the ancients' perspective on space was constrained. Is it not conceivable that we are merely seeing a small segment of time that operates much as the earth's horizon does, looping back around upon itself if we continue our journey far enough? If so, there would be no "first cause." Each event would merely be an equally valid cause (and effect), all links in an eternal chain.

Of course, even this is too simple a model. The chain of cause and effect isn't really a chain at all, but rather a tapestry of interconnected chains, with different "causes" intersecting with various degrees of relevance and interacting to form a vast array of "effects" … which, in turn, become causes in their own right.

Vast?

Infinite?

Perhaps. But again, we have no way of testing to be sure. What we *can* be sure of is it's the height of arrogance to simply dismiss the possibility of an infinite reality or a circular (spherical?) temporal model. Certainly there are very few perfectly straight lines in the universe, but there are myriad instances of the spherical form repeating itself in everything from buckyballs at the microscopic level through garden peas and oranges to planets, stars and even galaxies. None of this proves that time is, likewise, spherical. But it does indicate that we'd be foolhardy to dismiss the possibility, given the precedents that exist on the spatial plane.

Having dismissed the argument based on flawed premises, there's no real need to explore its other flaws.

But for those who find the above argument unconvincing, it should be pointed out that establishing a first cause is not the same as proving the existence of God. In fact, science has identified a possible first cause as something called a "big bang" — an event scientists claim to have pinpointed by extrapolating data backward and applying the laws of physics as we understand them. Not being a physicist, I can't presume to speak with any more specificity on the matter. Suffice to say, however, that the hypothesized big bang has virtually nothing in common with a supernatural voice emanating from a celestial megaphone and announcing with the appropriate pomp and gravity, "Let there be light! (Now! Goddammit!)"

The existence of such a "big bang," even if authenticated, doesn't necessarily preclude its identity as part of a cycle that involves periodic expansions and contractions of matter and energy, a potentially endless cycle that simply repeats itself ad infinitum. Again, we can't preclude the possibility of the infinite, because the entirety of reality is simply beyond our scope. If it *does* turn out to be infinite, we'll never know it, because we aren't equipped to observe it. But that doesn't mean we can assume it to be finite when it extends far beyond the reach of both our perception and understanding.

Science simply cannot resolve the question of whether the universe is infinite. But faith, on the other hand, pretends to have the answer — an answer that is, conveniently, impossible to verify. It's a shaky proposition at best.

Even assuming that the first cause were, in fact, a deity, we would still be unable to state with any certainty which deity (or convocation of deities) was responsible — or even whether the guilty party was a deity known to humanity. All the competing claims by all the theistic cultures throughout history and around the world are nothing but a cacophony of contradictions that produce no empirical evidence but, rather, a slew of unsupported hypotheses.

The Egyptians alone had several different creation myths, attributing the dirty deed to several different gods. In the Heliopolitan myth, Atum (Adam?) created the world through an act of masturbation. The priests of Memphis put Ptah, the artisan god, forward as their favored candidate. Thebans, meanwhile, maintained that Amun had created the world by uttering a call that is compared to the honk of a primeval goose. Khnum, the god of the Nile's headwaters, supposedly created the other deities and human beings on his potter's wheel.

If we don't like those options, we can cast our net further afield.

Do we cast our lot with Imra of the Hindu Kush, who created the gods of the Kafir pantheon by his breath? Or perhaps we prefer Mbombo, the central African god who vomited creation into being. Too messy for you? Why not try Awonawilona, creator of the world according to Zuni peoples of New Mexico. Or Pangu of China, who emerged from a primordial cosmic egg. If you prefer a feminine form, you might wish to consider Aditi, the "boundless one" and mother of all in the Indian Rigveda.

As often as not, gods work in conjunction with one another to create the world. In the Pacific Northwest, it is said that Raven created the world but could not fashion light. To do so, he paid a visit to the "house of light," where he transformed himself into a speck of dirt that was eventually swallowed by the woman who lived there. This impregnated her, and she gave birth to a child with the habit of playing with various bundles that adorned the walls. Each time he tired of one, it would float up through a smoke hole in the roof, creating in turn the stars, the moon and the sun.

In Mayan mythology, creation was the work of Tepeu ("sovereign") and Q'uq'umatz, the feathered serpent, who joined forces to think the world into being. In Genesis, we have evidence to indicate that a council of gods — the plural noun Elohim — created the world and declared, "Let *us* make mankind in *our* image and *our* likeness."

These are just a few of the myriad stories from which we must choose. And so we wind up right back where we started, deciding among any number of equally plausible — or implausible — scenarios with no real evidence upon which to base our decision.

Perhaps the possibilities themselves are infinite, but there's no way for us to know that, either, from our limited perspective. We are left, therefore, with nothing whatsoever upon which to base our conclusions.

If there's some small consolation in all this, it lies in the very concept that evades our grasp: the infinite. For if the universe *does* turn out to be truly infinite, the reality any one of us envisions is bound to manifest itself sooner or later. Suddenly, the crapshoot turns into a "can't lose" proposition. All paths lead to the top of the same mountain, as the saying goes. As author Neil Gaiman wrote in his novel InterWorld, "This is a work of fiction. Still, given an infinite number of possible worlds, it must be true on one of them. And if a story set in an infinite number of possible worlds is true in one of them, then it must be true in all of them. So maybe, it's not as fictional as we think."

The same could, conceivably, be said for the Bible or the Qur'an or any number of other religious texts.

The downside for the vain and self-important folks who take these works as gospel is that their reality won't be any more valid than anyone else's. Under such circumstances, its manifestation will be a small dish full of cold comfort to the "my way or the highway to hell" crowd. But I think I'll let them eat it alone; my appetite is for a richer sort of fare.

Eighteen: Fate or Freedom

When I was a few months shy of my seventeenth birthday, a Canadian band called Rush released an album (yes, they were still called pressed vinyl back then) called *Permanent Waves*. It opened with a rousing track called *The Spirit of Radio* that was the first single off the record, but it was the second track on Side One that caught my attention. It was a track called *Freewill*, with lyrics by the band's drummer, Neil Peart.

An anthem for free choice, it hit just the right note with a boy in his late teens ready — or so I thought — to start making his own decisions. Some of those decisions turned out to be glorious, while others turned out to be staggering missteps. I benefitted from the former, and I'm still feeling the effects from some of the latter.

The point is, however, that they were mine.

Or so I thought.

You can choose a ready guide in some celestial voice.
If you choose not to decide, you still have made a choice.
You can choose from phantom fears and kindness that can kill;

I will choose a path that's clear
I will choose Free Will.

Yet free will is hardly as simple as it might as first appear, in either practical or philosophical terms. From a practical standpoint, someone always seems hell-bent on depriving others of this precious commodity; from a philosophical standpoint, one must contend with the very real question of whether it even exists. It's somewhat convenient, however, that many of those who argue against it philosophically do so to bolster their own case for withholding it from others. This tendency has been apparent through virtually the entire history of Western monotheism, and examples of it are strewn across earlier pages in this present work.

Those who invoke the concept of determinism, free will's opposite number, often do so to "keep people in their place." Male chauvinists would confine women to apron strings and, in an earlier time, with chastity belts. Members of the highest social caste would cement the system in place, allowing movement neither up nor down a shattered social ladder. Churchmen would sentence the laity to a life of illiteracy, and kings would condemn their vassals to an existence of toil and servitude. Slaveholders would treat human beings as property to be bought and sold, defining each bondservant as some fraction of a person.

Is it any wonder that the Bible was used to justify slavery in the United States? When the New Testament commands slaves to "obey your earthly masters" — not once but twice — and the very core of Christian dogma describes all humanity as enslaved to sin, should we really expect anything different. The book of Ephesians even goes so far as to compare slaveholders, in some sense, to Christ. One can only imagine how Jesus himself might have reacted to such a comparison.

Slavery fits in very neatly with the idea of preserving the status quo, which the monotheists are always intent upon doing. Not only does it enable them to line their pockets with wealth produced by the toil of others, it also perpetuates the illusion that the world is safe and secure — the same yesterday, today and forever. Some slaves are slaves against their will, while others are slaves because they fear shaking off this comfortable illusion. The former are kept in their place by threats such as hell, excommunication or death; the latter by false promises of predictability.

The Hebrews of the Old Testament were held in thrall by kings. The most beloved of them, David and Solomon, were among the worst of the lot. David used his power to bed another man's wife, then arranged to have her husband slain in battle, thereby directly violating the commands against covetousness, deceit and murder in one fell swoop. Solomon, for his part, accumulated a vast harem and levied burdensome taxes for the purpose of building an extravagant temple to Yahweh. Ironically, the Bible fails to condemn him for these practices, instead focusing on his "sin" of idolatry in acknowledging Asherah, the ancient goddess consort of Yahweh.

It's fine to seek the truth, but one must seek it within the prescribed parameters. Just ask Galileo, for instance. Or consult Article 6 among the "Articles of Religion" adopted by the Church of England, which explicitly states that "Holy Scripture contains all things necessary to salvation." Or spend some time with today's evangelical Christians, who are likely to counsel you against exposing yourself to college classes that teach evolution, secular music and yoga (for starters). Other traditions even go so far as to forbid blood transfusions or visits to a physician, on the ground that such exercises betray a lack of faith.

In the context of Christianity, the issue can be traced back to Paul's idea of original sin, which has been challenged repeatedly as both cruel and unjust at various points in church history but has always emerged victorious. The Gnostics issued such a challenge when they claimed that spiritual knowledge, not the human sacrifice of a god-man, was the true path to salvation. They quickly found their beliefs at first suppressed and, eventually, all but forgotten. One can't help but notice, however, that the prospect of knowledge —

whether scientific or spiritual — obtained through individual study always constitutes a threat to those in power. The masses must be constrained within those prescribed parameters, lest they "see with their eyes, hear with their ears, understand in their hearts and turn to be healed" (Isaiah 6:10). No, we can't have that. The same sort of people who frowned on the pursuit of gnosis in the third century would be harping on the evils of "secular education" in the 21st.

As the Gnostics were on the verge of fading into history, another challenge emerged in the person of a British ascetic who dared to deny the doctrine of original sin. He directed his critique primarily at our old friend Augustine, whose teachings on original sin — Pelagius pointed out quite rationally — would condemn men to hell for doing something they could not avoid. For his trouble, he was banished from Rome and his writings were destroyed. His views survive today in the form of quotations by his opponents and remain the subject of condemnation today. The Anglican Articles of Religion referenced above also contain a casually self-righteous declaration that "the Pelagians do vainly talk."

If there had ever been any doubt about which way the issue of freedom vs. determinism would be decided, it all but ended there. Whereas Pelagius' writings were destroyed, Augustine's became more widely disseminated than any other religious text of their time save the Bible itself. The Catholics declared him one of thirty-three "doctors of the church," men whose writings are deemed timeless expressions of orthodox theology. He is revered not only by Catholics, but by Protestants as well and may be among the three most influential religious writers in the West — along with Paul and Muhammad.

His influence can be keenly felt in the later writings of men like Martin Luther and John Calvin, both of whom echoed his affinity for determinism (and, by extension, his contempt for the concept of free will). Luther argued that God's grace was necessary for salvation, and Calvin took this idea to its logical conclusion: that individuals are predestined for either heaven or damnation from all eternity. Those in the former group, known as "The Elect," are supposedly the only ones for whom Jesus' atonement has any effect. It's not hard to recognize this as simply another variation on the "chosen people" theme that enables insecure believers in this or that theology to feel superior to those who aren't lucky enough to be part of the "in crowd."

This so-called doctrine of limited atonement is one of the five points of Calvinism into which his ideas have been distilled. The other four are:

1. Total depravity — just another phrase to describe the utter hopeless condition of slavery imposed on humanity by Adam's "original sin."

2. Unconditional election — the idea that salvation is based on God's grace alone and has nothing to do with good deeds or virtuous intent. It's the equivalent of receiving an automatic raise from your employer rather than getting a merit-based bonus.

3. Irresistible grace — if God wants to save you, there's nothing you can do to prevent it.

4. Perseverance of the saints — since it's impossible for a human being to thwart God's will, it's similarly impossible for anyone to truly "fall away" from the faith; rather, the Elect remain in communion with God eternally.

Whereas Augustine was challenged by Pelagius, the 16th century determinists — Luther in particular — found themselves criticized by Erasmus of Rotterdam, who argued for a greater degree of freedom than they were willing to allow. Erasmus wrote a work titled *The Freedom of the Will*, and Luther countered with one called *On the Bondage of the Will*. Erasmus had reason on his side, and his works remain highly respected today in certain circles. Yet the much more widely known names and doctrines of Luther and Calvin testify effectively as to who came out the winner.

If we learn nothing else from studying the tensions between freedom and security through the centuries, it should be obvious that security has the upper hand. Ironically, we may have one of Darwin's fundamental principles to thank for this. If the fundamental goal of all life is to perpetuate itself — to survive and reproduce — then this goal must supersede the impulse for freedom. Even the illusion of security is a more powerful draw for us than the promise of adventure. As Abraham Maslow demonstrated with his hierarchy of needs, it's difficult to focus on the arts and intellectual development when one is preoccupied with the needs for food and shelter. Or even sex. Adventures are for the fit and philosophical, not for the downtrodden and destitute.

The powers that be not only have a vested interest in keeping the masses enslaved, they have the means at their disposal — wealth, literacy, prestige — to persuade them that their slavery is in fact a form of security. But security, while among the most fundamental human needs, is also by very virtue of this fact the lowest common denominator. It's almost as though humanity is engaged in a perpetual cycle of rising above this lowest of possible expectations, only to slip inexorably backward until spurred once more to action. The United States was founded by individuals who sought, among other things, the freedom to worship as — or if — the pleased. It was founded by an odd mix of Deists, Puritans and atheists (among others) who wrote a constitution guaranteeing freedom of religion. Yet today, more than two centuries later, a significant and very vocal segment of this same country's citizens insist that it was founded on "biblical principles" as a "Christian nation" and imply — sometimes even stating explicitly — that it should be governed by the laws of their god rather than by the will of the people.

As D.H. Lawrence wrote, "Men fight for liberty and win it with hard knocks. Their children, brought up easy, let it slip away again, poor fools. And their grandchildren are once more slaves."

Scientific Determinations

When all the filth of hidden agendas and controlling theology is stripped away, however, one must address, at least in passing, the concept of scientific determinism. If we take gods out of the equation, we must ask ourselves (if we wish to be honest) whether we are not still enslaved to some form of destiny. Are we not merely threads in a vast three-dimensional tapestry of cause and effect, bound to follow the course set before us by an unimaginably complex nexus of interdependent events?

Some mathematical and philosophical models indicate that this may, indeed, be the case.

Yet for those less disposed to the idea of being a lump of clay or a thread in a tapestry — or preprogrammed computer chip — hope remains. A crucial element in Darwin's model is the occurrence of mutations, unpredicted variations that alter the course of evolution. Without them, in fact, evolution itself could not occur. Species could not adapt. And life itself could therefore not exist for long, being doomed to extinction the minute its environment changed to any appreciable degree.

Is such mutation truly random? And if so, is such randomness the basis for the existence of free will? Some evidence from quantum physics would seem to indicate that there's more to our universe than linear or even three-dimensional causation. There are so many things out there that we don't understand, discoveries yet to be made that could rock the foundations of our current understanding every bit as much as those of Edison or Galileo.

We can dismiss contradictions that are known to us, but we can't dismiss the possibility of new discoveries that could radically alter our perspective. Hence the title of this book: *Requiem for a Phantom God.* It is written not to discredit any conception of deity, but rather to free us from the chains of self-contradiction that bind us to a particular and nonsensical view of the divine. Once this god has been left behind, we are free to search the cosmos and our inner selves to find whatever might lie out there … and within. Whether we call it god or something else is actually beside the point.

Jesus is quoted as saying in the Gospel of Thomas: "If those who lead you say to you, 'See, the kingdom is in heaven,' then the birds of heaven will precede you. If they say to you, 'It is in the sea,' then the fish of the sea will precede you. But the kingdom of heaven is within you, and it is outside you. When you know yourselves, then you will be known, and you will know that you are sons of the living father. But if you do not know yourselves, you live in poverty, and you are poverty."

"I do not feel obliged to believe that the same God who has endowed us with sense, reason, and intellect has intended us to forgo their use."

— Galileo Galilei

To an Unknown God

If you take with you only two ideas from this modest tome, I'd ask that you remember the following.

1. You must choose between immanence and transcendence. It's impossible to have a god who is both "good" and the creator of all things — those which we call good on one hand and evil on the other. Any attempt to reconcile these totally irreconcilable concepts will result in one of two things: a god who is, to reference C.S. Lewis, a self-contradictory exercise in nonsense, or a system of morality that is meaningless, capricious and, ultimately, *amoral*. Neither outcome, in my view, is acceptable.

2. Our gods, if we choose to believe in them, must be forced to live up to ethics that far surpass our own human standards. If they fall short of the ethical conditions we place upon ourselves,

what use are they to us — except to help us rationalize our own failures?

Making the choice between the tribal and universal gods can be difficult. It's always tempting to believe we've got someone with unlimited power on our side. Think of it in terms of athletics. Many Christians will pray the "politically correct" prayer to the transcendent god before a game: Protect the players on both sides from injury and ensure the contest is a fair one. God is not seen as favoring either side. Yet if NFL quarterback Tim Tebow and pro basketball guard Jeremy Lin — two high-profile Christian athletes — perform well, their fans see it on some level as validation of their belief system. Before you know it, they've abandoned the universal god who doesn't take sides for the jealous god who turns up the wrath on his perceived enemies. Some may remember the Old Testament showdown between Elijah and Baal, a no-holds-barred death match complete with lightning bolts as weapons. When Baal was a no-show, 450 of his prophets paid the price ... with their lives.

Monotheists seek validation on a philosophical level, as well.

Champions of monotheism have depicted it as the apex in a process of cultural evolution (they'll use that word when it suits them) from animism to polytheism and, finally, to the belief in a single god. This model makes two related assumptions: One is that the monotheistic model is more modern than the others, and the second is that it is somehow superior.

When one considers that monotheism arose at a point in history when monarchs ruled the land, one has to wonder at the former statement. Monarchies have, by and large, gone the way of the dinosaur; the majority that survive are constitutional monarchies, in which kings and queens are little more than ceremonial figureheads. They're retained as goodwill ambassadors or symbols of a nation's identity, but practically speaking, they're about as functional and necessary as a person's appendix or wisdom teeth. If we're talking in terms of evolution, the monarchial system is largely an antiquated, vestigial structure.

It's telling that the only remaining pure (non-constitutional) monarchy in Europe can be found in Vatican City, where the pope stands guard over a monotheist state. Most of the other remaining absolute or near-absolute monarchies can be found in places where the Islamic version of monotheism is the state religion. While the number of pure monarchies can be counted on two hands, the number of democracies (representative, parliamentary and other forms) can be counted at between slightly fewer than and somewhat more than one hundred.

One could argue that polytheism resembles democracy far more closely and is therefore a more "advanced" system of belief. It's certainly not as prone to holy wars, because it's not based on an "us vs. them" mentality. Monotheism has a built in prejudice that says, "My god exists, but your god is a phony pretender." The upshot of this is, "My god can do whatever he damn well pleases, because he made the rules. I reserve the right to condemn the same atrocities you sanction in the name of your god that I commit in the name of mine."

This is why the same people who condemn the Holocaust or the Armenian Genocide can defend the very same sort of behavior committed by Old Testament kings and priests in the name of the Hebrew god. It's why the same lawmakers who deny a place to Muslim Sharia law in U.S. courthouses fight tooth and nail to post copies of the Jewish Ten Commandments in these very same buildings. When allegiance to one god or another trumps ethics and principles that should transcend religion, the result is chaos, bitterness and, ultimately, murder.

Part of the problem is that some religions want to claim these transcendent principles as uniquely their own. Many Christians, for instance, view the "Golden Rule" as a uniquely inspired teaching of Jesus, either not realizing or refusing to acknowledge that similar sentiments have been attributed to Confucius, the rabbi Hillel and others who lived prior to Jesus. Today, they're to be found in

Brahmanism, Buddhism, Hinduism, Jainism, Taoism, Wicca and Zoroastrianism, to name a few.

Monotheists all too often view themselves as the sole arbiters of truth and are more than willing to resort to violence as a means of "proving" their point.

As Isaac Asmiov once declared, "Violence is the last refuge of the incompetent."

Incompetence is hardly limited to monotheists. And atrocities have certainly been committed in polytheistic — and democratic — states. Primitive cultures murdered men, women and children to serve as "sacrifices" to their deities. They marched into battle with one another under the banners of their war gods. They shouted at the top of their lungs, "Our god's way is the right way!" But they didn't scream, "Our god's way is the *only* way!"

There's a subtle difference between these two attitudes. The first promotes conquest and subjugation; the second advocates extermination. The Romans conquered vast territories but allowed the continued worship of local gods, so long as such worship did not undermine the rule of Rome. The empire even promoted local deities and built temples in their honor. Herod the Great, the client king of Judea installed and supported by Rome, undertook just such a project when he sought to build an elaborate temple to the Jewish god. Temples and statues dedicated to Roman gods stood side-by-side with those honoring local deities, neither being considered superior to the other. Modern Americans whose cars are adorned with "Coexist" bumper stickers would have certainly felt at home. Indeed, so inclusive were the Romans that the biblical Book of Acts reports that Paul, in his travels, came across an altar in Athens inscribed with the words TO AN UNKNOWN GOD. Talk about covering all your bases.

Several non-Roman gods were worshipped widely throughout the empire. Among them were the Egyptian goddess Isis, whose "black virgin" statues have been found not only in North Africa but across Europe, as well as the Persian god Mithra, who became popular within the Roman armed forces.

It wasn't the Romans who made trouble for observant Jews around the time of Jesus, but the other way around. To be sure, any subjugated nation is bound to feel resentment toward its conqueror. Still, the empire would have been perfectly content to allow the continuance of Jewish worship alongside the reverence for other gods. It was the monotheists, with their insistence on exclusivity, who would have none of this. Other gods simply could not be recognized in any way, shape or form.

This elitist mentality carried over into Christianity, with its pogroms against heathens and heretics. Compare the "live and let live" policy of Rome to Augustine's approach of forced conversions and tell me which is more humane. Or civilized. Or, for that matter, more worthy of Jesus, who welcomed tax gatherers and "sinners" while counseling against precisely the sort of judgmentalism practiced by his successors.

Religion or Cult?

The idea that monotheism is somehow superior to other forms of theism is based, it seems, solely on the number of worshippers willing to advocate in its behalf. In point of fact, this "strength in numbers" bias seems to be all that separates a respected religious practice from a sect or cult.

In his book *Popular Psychology*, Dr. Luis Cordon of Eastern Connecticut State University identifies six elements of coercive persuasion — otherwise known as brainwashing — each of which could easily be applied not only to cults, but also to elements of orthodox Christian doctrine:

1. Application of physical or emotional distress.

While most mainstream churches don't apply such distress directly, they do take advantage of stressful situations that are already present. Many churches recruit heavily in poor neighborhoods and send missionaries to impoverished areas where they can recruit those grateful for their help. As a recent example, missionaries were drawn to Haiti after an earthquake in early 2010 devastated that already impoverished country.

An Associated Press article from February of that year put it this way: "Baptists, Catholics, Jehovah's Witnesses, Scientologists, Mormons and other missionaries have flocked to Haiti in droves since the earthquake — feeding the homeless, treating the injured *and preaching the Gospel* in squalid camps where some 1 million people now live" (emphasis added).

Meanwhile, televangelist Pat Robertson was labeling the earthquake God's judgment upon the island nation for supposedly entering into a "pact with the devil" centuries earlier. This sounds uncomfortably like the "old good cop, bad cop" routine — Christian missionaries provided needed aid, while one of their leaders invoked the fear of punishment for some act committed long before any of quake victims were born — if it was committed at all.

Sound familiar?

Meanwhile, ten members of a Christian missionary group were charged with taking 33 children from their Haitian families and trying to relocate them in an orphanage across the border in the Dominican Republic. Charges against nine of the group members were dropped, and the leader was convicted of a lesser charge before being freed for time served.

Regardless, the question remains: How far are missionaries from recognized churches prepared to go in their attempts to "win the world for Christ." Is it a form of bribery to offer aid in exchange for the opportunity to preach the gospel? At the very least, isn't it a conflict of interest?

The same sort of tactic has long been a favorite of populist politicians, many of whom have risen to power by offering material help in exchange for votes. New York's Tammany Hall political machine, for instance, was known to provide rental assistance, food and jobs to immigrants in exchange for their support at the polls. How is this different from offering the same sort of essential aid in exchange for the opportunity to preach one's particular brand of religious dogma?

2. One simple explanation.

The doctrine of original sin fits that description perfectly. This "simple" explanation is a lot easier to swallow than the complex factors that actually give rise to most problems. The preacher then repeats the explanation so often that believing it becomes almost second nature. Humanity is guilty and unworthy of God's great love. *You* are unworthy of God's great love. You are cursed. Guilty. A wretched sinner. Repeat ten times every hour and write it a hundred times on the blackboard during detention. Then maybe you can go home for the day.

The "good news" is that simple problems can be resolved with simple solutions, such as Jesus dying on the cross for your sins. This simplicity is welcomed by the person in the midst of life's stresses and trials, because it provides a convenient distraction from those more pressing, real-life problems: illness, addiction, debt, divorce, unemployment.

The bad news is that such a "solution" won't solve any of those problems. It will merely compound them while you wait for divine intervention to whisk them all away.

3. Unconditional love, acceptance and attention.

This fits the orthodox Christian model perfectly as well. Jesus is presented as the embodiment of unconditional love. All that is required is that one "believe." Ethics and principles are dispensable — or even inconvenient when they conflict with the message of obedience; the only thing that matters is an expression of faith. Once the leader of the movement (the person claiming to represent Jesus) has your faith, he can exploit it to his own advantage … and for his own purposes.

4. Creation of a new identity.

Here, the Bible can be quoted directly: "If therefore anyone is in Christ, he is a new creation. The old has passed away, and the new has arrived" (2 Cor. 5:17). The identity, of course, is not that of an individual, but rather a reflection of the group leader. A clone, a zombie or a dittohead.

In the words of Paul, "All of you who were baptized into Christ have clothed yourself in Christ" (Gal. 3:27). What actually happens, however, is that followers get baptized into the teachings *about* Christ promoted by a man in a robe or three-piece suit on the pulpit.

5. Entrapment: the foot-in-the door technique.

The demands made upon a member are initially small, but they are gradually increased until they become intolerable. By this time, however, the recruit is either too deeply invested or too frightened of the consequences to turn back.

Churches may attract new members with rhetoric about unconditional love, but conditions are added all too soon. Members must abstain from alcohol. They must knock on doors and attempt to recruit more followers. They must attend church regularly, wear certain kinds of attire and indoctrinate their children. The penalty for failing to live up to such expectations? A one-way ticket to hell, not to mention exile from the "body" of Christ. The cancer, after all, must be removed before it affects the rest of the "members."

6. Limited access to information.

Group members are cut off from their previous support system, and critical thinking is discouraged. Members are told to stay away from "secular" ideas, because "the devil prowls around like a roaring lion, looking for someone to devour."

Members are further discouraged from thinking for themselves, because the devil can deceive those "proud" enough to trust their own intellect rather than placing their unquestioning faith in the Bible and its appointed guardians — the clergy.

In the Dark Ages, access to information was limited by destroying all writings deemed heretical and perpetuating a climate of illiteracy across Europe. It's one thing to depend upon a priesthood to interpret holy scripture. But it's even more effective when they can't read it in the first place. They might actually get it into their heads that "love thy neighbor" is more important than "pay your tithes."

All this leaves us with very little to distinguish established monotheism from its cultish cousins. The main difference, it would seem, is that one has more adherents than the other. It's simply a matter of popularity. Members of the established church glorify their own actions though the use of appealing language, while in the next breath condemning the very same sorts of actions on the part of so-called cults.

If a Christian claims a wondrous supernatural event, it's called a miracle; if someone outside the Christian tradition does so, it's dismissed as the work of "demons." If millions of people believe in something, they've got faith; if a few hundred believe in precisely the same sort of thing, they're the victims of brainwashing or psychological manipulation.

Can someone please enlighten me as to how threats of eternal punishment are any less manipulative than the kind of strong-arm tactics employed by people like Jim Jones? Is it because hell is just a bluff, while the murderous control Jones exerted over his followers was all too real?

Why is Jesus lauded for sending his inner circle out to "make disciples of all nations" while Hare Krishnas are derided as pests in airports? And what about those bike-riding Mormon missionaries and pamphlet-loving Jehovah's Witnesses? Where do they fall along the spectrum?

Why is it more acceptable for Jesus to demand that his disciples turn against their own families than it is for a radical cult leader to do the same? Is it because Jesus has more followers? What makes it more acceptable for Christians to revel in the concept of an apocalyptic war than it is for cult members to quit their jobs, sell everything they own and climb to the top of a mountain expecting aliens to land there and whisk them away? After all, even Jesus told that rich young man to sell everything he had and "come, follow me."

The difference lies not in the acts themselves or the principles behind them, but merely in the fact that millions have endorsed them in one form and spurned them in another.

It's called hypocrisy — the very thing Jesus himself condemned in the strongest of terms.

Adventures Await

The universe is full of wonders. If we ascribe them to the hand of a god, that makes them no more wonderful, and if we see no divine hand at work in them, it diminishes them not a whit. The majesty of the ocean waves or the mighty sequoia join the marvels of a hummingbird in flight and the amazing capacity of the human heart to inspire us and challenge us to become better than we are.

Yes, to evolve.

It's not a dirty word. We can sit with our collective head in the sand and quake in fear of the desert storm that may be approaching. Or, alternatively, we can strike out with the next caravan on an adventure that may lead us to an oasis, a shining city or … yes … that much-feared sandstorm. The storms will always come, but it is our choice whether to go. Those who seek to deprive us of this choice are those who seek to enslave us, and it matters not whether they do so on their own accord or whether they attribute their actions to an almighty god.

Taking a god's name in vain is not simply a matter of avoiding the words "God damn it!" when you stub your toe on some door you've left ajar. It's a matter of misrepresenting your own actions as the "will of God" and seeking to impose that will on others. I find it hard to imagine a more blatant violation of the edict against bearing false witness. Those are two of the commandments right there, and if you use them as a basis for condoning murder or theft … well, as the saying goes, three strikes and you're out.

People have been presuming to speak in the name of God for millennia. And still others have presumed to speak in the name of others who have presumed to speak in the name of God. Several books by otherwise anonymous writers made their way into the Christian canon on the strength of their supposed authorship, only to have that authorship questioned when modern scholars compared their writing styles more closely. Among the most famous is the Epistle to the Hebrews, long credited to Paul — and probably included in the New Testament largely on this basis — but now known to be the work of an anonymous author.

Identity theft? Today we would say so. But back then, it was common practice.

Indeed, nearly half of the letters attributed to Paul are doubted to be his, and the authorship of virtually all the so-called Catholic epistles in the canon has similarly been questioned. The idea that Moses wrote the five books attributed to him is largely dismissed on the basis of their varying styles and the fact that Moses' own death is described in their pages. Various books under the name of Solomon were also in wide circulation during Jesus' day, though they were written long after his death. The Wisdom, Odes, Psalms and other volumes were read in addition to three books in the Old Testament collection. The old admonition to "consider the source" can hardly be followed when one has no idea what — or who — the source is.

With so many variables and so few scruples involved, is there really any point in attempting to separate the truth from the misrepresentation? Aren't we better off simply listening to the voice of our own compassion? There's no reason to give someone claiming to speak for God any more credence than someone purporting to speak in his own behalf. Indeed, the person who prefaces his advice to me with "thus sayeth the Lord!" has just invited a far greater degree of scrutiny — if I even have the time and energy to bother with it. The word of a god should speak for itself; it shouldn't have to be promoted ad nauseam through some dogmatic megaphone. If it is, I grow suspicious … and you should, too.

When theists confront me with messages they claim to have received from God, I assess them by asking the same questions I ask when anyone else sets a proposal before me:

1. Who benefits, and how?
2. Does it violate my personal code of ethics?
3. Can it be defended rationally?

If the answer to any one of these questions fails to meet with my satisfaction, there's no point in wasting further energy on it.

Perhaps that sounds cold.

To me, it simply clears my schedule to deal with more important things … such as loving my family, feeling and expressing compassion, creating and appreciating beauty, and exploring the wonders of the universe. This last is what led me to pursue the questions addressed in this book. Whether you agree with the answers I have provided is immaterial if I've encouraged you, in some way, to continue your own fearless quest for understanding. True understanding leaves no place for bigotry or condemnation — which are but stumbling blocks to waylay us on our journey. It is a journey ever forward on a road paved with change and opportunity. We need no voices crying in the wilderness to prepare the way before us, but only our own open minds and open hearts.

This, to me, is the good news.

It is nothing less than the meaning of life.

Also by the author

Works of Fiction
The Memortality Saga
Memortality
Paralucidity
Academy of the Lost Labyrinth
The Talismans of Time
Pathfinder of Destiny
The Only Dragon
Identity Break
Feathercap
Nightmare's Eve
Crimson Scourge

Works of Nonfiction
A Whole Different League
The Great American Shopping Experience
California's Historic Highways series
Highway 99
Highway 101
America's Historic Highways series
America's First Highways
Yesterday's Highways
Highways of the South
Highways of the West series
America's Loneliest Road
Victory Road

The Lincoln Highway in California
(with Gary Kinst)
Roadside Illustrated series
    Happy Motoring!
    Signpost Up Ahead: The East
    Signpost Up Ahead: The West
Mark Twain's Nevada
The Century Cities series (10 books)
Fresno Growing Up
Martinsville Memories
The Legend of Molly Bolin
50 Undefeated
The Phoenix Chronicles
    The Osiris Testament
    The Way of the Phoenix
    The Gospel of the Phoenix
The Phoenix Principle
    Forged in Ancient Fires
    Messiah in the Making

"We must question the story logic of having an
all-knowing all-powerful God, who creates faulty humans,
and then blames them for his own mistakes."
— Gene Roddenberry

Stephen H. Provost

The author writes about American highways, mutant superheroes, mythic archetypes and pretty much anything he wants. A journalist, historian, philosopher and novelist, he lives in Northern Nevada. And he loves cats. Read his blogs and keep up with his latest activities at stephenhprovost.com.